HISTORICAL ARCHAEOLOGY

But nothing's lost. Or else: all is translation
And every bit of us is lost in it
—James Merrill, "Lost in Translation"

For Paul A. Shackel

Historical Archaeology

Why the Past Matters

Barbara J. Little

Routledge
Taylor & Francis Group

LONDON AND NEW YORK

First published 2007 by Left Coast Press, Inc.

Published 2016 by Routledge
2 Park Square, Milton Park, Abingdon, Oxon OX14 4RN
711 Third Avenue, New York, NY 10017, USA

Routledge is an imprint of the Taylor & Francis Group, an informa business

Library of Congress Cataloguing-in-Publication Information

Little, Barbara J.
    Historical archaeology : why the past matters / Barbara J. Little.
        p. cm.
    Includes bibliographical references and index.
    ISBN-13: 978-1-59874-022-6 (hardcover : alk. paper)
    ISBN-10: 1-59874-022-9 (hardcover : alk. paper)
    ISBN-13: 978-1-59874-023-3 (paperback : alk. paper)
    ISBN-10: 1-59874-023-7 (paperback : alk. paper)
    1. Archaeology and history. 2. Historic sites. 3. Excavations (Archaeology)
    4. Archaeology—Philosophy. 5. Archaeology—Methodology. I. Title.
    CC77.H5L58 2007
    930.1—dc22   2006026623

ISBN-13: 978-1-59874-022-6 (hardcover)
ISBN-13: 978-1-59874-023-3 (paperback)

Contents

Section 4: Historical Archaeology as Public Scholarship

List of Figures

Preface

I **wrote this book** because I have been interested in how often we say that we value history because we learn from the past. I have been deeply impressed by how little we actually seem to do so.

I also am fascinated by the ways that we seem to connect only with selected parts of the past. Often our selective memory seems to focus on our own specific (selected) ancestors and, more troubling, on those parts of the past that we use to reassure ourselves that things are as they should be. In other words, I find it troubling, if unsurprising, that the past is used to support the status quo, with all its intolerance, injustice, and inequality. I believe we can do better.

The past provides us with a long-term perspective. For those with a scientific bent, it may be useful to think of it as a laboratory of sorts, albeit a rather sloppy one, where humanity has tried out many different approaches to living in the human condition. Our scholarship—our penchant for studying and analyzing—can help us to move beyond lip service to an ability to truly learn from the past and from other cultures. In addition, hopefully, we can also act on the lessons we learn. We are a global village full of conflict, cooperation, and certainties that are anything but certain. Prejudice and fear arise from lies, misperceptions, and partial truths.

As a child growing up during the Cold War, I watched countless hours of TV programming about spies, law and order, and justice. That courtroom phrase "the truth, the whole truth, and nothing but the truth" resonated with me. I came to believe that the whole story matters and I still believe it. We sometimes live up to the "better angels of our nature," as Abraham Lincoln put it in his first inaugural address. At the other extreme, sometimes we create—and even revel in—injustice, terror, and chaos.

We tend to ignore evidence in favor of what we think we know or want to believe. I believe that we need a different attitude. Documentary history offers us one set of evidence about the past. Archaeology offers us a different kind of evidence. Historical archaeology is a kind of scholarship that challenges our certainties in useful ways.

Many of my examples of historical archaeology—from Jamestown to the Garbage Project—come from the United States, which led the development of the discipline through the 20th century. Recently historical archaeology has boomed in other countries. I also include examples from Canada, England, Australia, Brazil, Ireland, and Ghana. Historical archaeology's focus on the development of the modern world insists that our work be global. I believe that we are starting to figure out how to balance the local against the global, general trends and far-reaching events against details, material against imagined.

We are learning about people's lives as they struggled and coped with variable success with the dramatic changes in the world over the last few centuries. And we are also learning more general things such as: people do things differently from what they say they do; everyday objects are important parts of our lives; diversity is the rule rather than the exception; humility and compassion are the most honest ways to approach our world. You will draw other conclusions from the work I explore here. One thing will surely strike you: ambiguity is pervasive; there is always more to the story.

Acknowledgments

It is no small logistical matter to write a book while one is working full time, so I'm a little amazed that I am at the point of writing acknowledgments. (Thanks to my coworkers, who tolerated my taking more vacation days than usual.)

I am heartened by how difficult it was to choose which stories to tell, particularly in section 3, because it speaks to me of how vibrant the field of historical archaeology has become over the last few decades. To my many colleagues who are not quoted or whose work is not featured, I apologize for my egregious lack of good judgment. It goes without saying, but I'll say it anyway: errors in interpretation are solely my responsibility.

I owe a great many thanks to:

Mitch Allen at Left Coast Press, especially because writing something like this has been on my mind for a while (and thanks for the ridiculously quick deadlines!—no, really. By the way, I still like my original title better);

Rachel Fudge, for her efficient and friendly production skills, and Angela Watrous for copyediting;

Bonnie Styles and Terry Martin of the Illinois State Museum for giving me a place to work during the second half of July 2005 where I could get seriously started writing this;

Friends and colleagues willing to talk about what the past means to them and archaeologists everywhere who see their work as meaningful;

Teresa Moyer, Paul Shackel, and Frank McManamon for their helpful comments, guide to resources, collegiality, and generous willingness to read the first draft quickly. Thanks to Frank McManamon for pointing out the complexity of the Henry Ford quote, and special thanks to Teresa Moyer for her fine editorial sense in uncovering snags in the final draft;

My colleagues who provided images: Stephen Brighton (Five Points), Bonnie McEwen and Elyse Cornelison (San Luis), Thad Van Bueren (Alabama Gates Camp), Paul Shackel (Harpers Ferry and New Philadelphia), Tom Durand of the National Park Service Historic Photo Collection (Jamestown);

Reviewers who have vastly improved this book: many very special thanks to Bob Paynter, Liz Brumfiel, and Mark Warner, and two anonymous reviewers, and also to a handful of anonymous Mills College undergraduates whose readings and comments were quite eye-opening;

Matt Burns for providing the music (or, more accurately, sharing the groove); and the all-hours waitresses at the Tastee Diner in Silver Spring who kept the refills coming.

Special thanks to Suheil Bushrui for his compassionate, inspired, and inspiring scholarship and commitment to the cause of peace.

I dedicate this book to Paul—husband, friend, intellectual partner—for courage in the struggle for peace and justice.

CHAPTER 1

Do History and Historical Archaeology Matter?

History is more or less bunk. It's tradition. We don't want tradition. We want to live in the present, and the only history that is worth a tinker's damn is the history we make today.

—HENRY FORD

In 1916, the *Chicago Tribune* reported this now-famous quote by industrialist Henry Ford. In shortened form—"history is bunk"—it has become a catchphrase for the forward-looking, history-disparaging viewpoint of the industrial age. But a little more context, of both the quote and Ford's life, is in order. The *Tribune* reporter was questioning Ford's lack of support for the buildup of American military forces and used a historical analogy about the defeat of Napoleon. Ford responded, "I don't know whether Napoleon did or did not try to get across there (to England) and I don't care. I don't know much about history, and I wouldn't give a nickel for all the history in the world. It means nothing to me. History is more or less bunk...."

The year 1916 was in the middle of World War I and all the knowledge of history in Europe did not stop that horror. Perhaps Ford was skeptical of history that didn't seem to make any difference at all. He was also interested in the history of ordinary people but didn't find it in the texts of the time or, presumably, in his rudimentary education. Ford is famous for, among other things, founding The Henry Ford Museum and Greenfield Village in Dearborn, Michigan. He collected everyday materials and buildings to promote the kind of history he thought was important (not to mention to counter the disapproving public perception of him as uneducated and ignorant of history). The mission statement of the museum today reads, "The Henry Ford provides unique educational experiences based on authentic objects, stories, and lives from America's traditions of ingenuity, resourcefulness, and innovation. Our purpose is to inspire people to learn from these traditions to help shape a better future." I don't want to overstate Henry Ford's commitment to a democratizing history, but his museum certainly has had an influence. Historical archaeology—as the archaeological study of historically documented time periods—holds a similar ambition to add "the rest of us" to history and to make that history useful.

The turn of the millennium encouraged a great deal of stocktaking around the world: looking to the future and looking back to gain perspective and lessons from the past. The interest in heritage that has been growing worldwide over the past few decades is currently booming, and it is not likely to be a passing fad. Archaeological sites and collections are part of our heritage, both globally and locally. Historical archaeologists combine the methods of both history and archaeology. We study both documents and material remains to investigate the past. For the most part, the past we study concerns the development of the modern world.

In some ways, America has been celebrating its newness since the first colonists came ashore. The mythical "New World" erased the shackles of European history, creating a blank slate from which a new society could emerge. Americans in general like to think of themselves as more comfortable with the future than with the past. Such perceptions clearly affect the ways that we value history and archaeology.

Generations of historians and archaeologists have been frustrated by an apparently deep-seated lack of interest or knowledge concerning the past among American citizens. We are frequently confronted with the results of some new poll that demonstrates how little Americans know about national history. A Harris Poll on Americans' knowledge about archaeology shows how hard it is, for example, for archaeologists to shake their widely assumed, erroneous association with dinosaurs.

Such examples, however, may be misleading. Americans may not know many details about the past, but at the same time we are intensely interested. The boom of interest in heritage over the last few decades has shown this other side of public interest. The Harris Poll reveals some of the surprising things that Americans believe about archaeology. For example, on a scale of 1 to 10, respondents rated the importance of archaeology to today's society a 7.3 and to understanding the modern world a 7.1. The poll's conclusions summarize findings about what Americans know and think about archaeology and highlight two key points that tie together the contradictory forces of a booming interest in the past and an intense interest in the future. First, "Archaeology is important because we improve the future by learning about the past." Second, "Archaeology helps us understand the modern world" (Ramos and Duganne 2000:31). These are extraordinary things for Americans to believe. Those who profess to believe these things are the same Americans who, in general, can't quite place Abraham Lincoln's presidency during the Civil War (see, for example, Neal and Martin 2000). The connection that Americans feel with the past also has been documented through a national telephone survey reported upon by public historians Roy Rosenzweig and David Thelen. They found that Americans see the past as a "reservoir of alternatives to the present." Their summary of what they see as a general perspective on the past is an eloquent expression about the sophisticated needs and expectations of the American public. They write:

> By recovering things from the past or by looking at experience differently we can see how to think and act differently in the future. The past can challenge us with eloquent, brilliant, troubling material that widens our present experience and wisdom. It provides perspectives to engage, accounts to cross-examine, and opportunities to hone skills of empathy, compassion, and reflection. (1998:205)

The past—or, more accurately, how we view and use the past—then, is an important part of our modern life. What we learn from history, whether documentary or archaeological, can shape our attitudes and relationships. It has the potential to inspire us as well as chasten us.

Sankofa is an Akan (Ghana) word that refers to the concept of reclaiming the past and understanding how the present came to be so that we can move forward. It came into the lexicon of archaeology through the African Burial Ground project in lower Manhattan where archaeologists and skeletal biologists excavated and analyzed a large graveyard from the 1700s. One of the coffin lids had tacks arranged in a heart shape that resembled the symbol for *sankofa*. Whatever the original intent of the coffin maker, the symbol invokes an idea. *Sankofa* is a useful concept for thinking about the way that we can relate the past to our current and future needs.

Sankofa implies that our interest in the past is drawn from our circumstances in the present and our hopes for the future. The questions we ask as historical archaeologists are inspired in the same way. I am, for example, fascinated by the challenges in promoting interest in and caring about "someone else's past" within an increasingly diverse population. Historical archaeology offers opportunities for us to become aware of our common humanity and our common struggles. In the face of cynicism and despair, archaeology can offer glimpses into the human story as a source of hope and renewal. We can all hope that respect—at least tolerance but perhaps even celebration—will flow from the present to the past and back again to the present.

The question of who owns the past has been raised time and again in the context of the modern preservation and heritage movements. Some dismiss this question as a paradox that cannot be resolved, while others are far more emphatic in affirming that the past belongs to everyone. The United Nations Educational, Scientific and Cultural Organization (UNESCO), for example, is clear that civilization is made up of contributions from all peoples and that all humanity shares a common heritage. Federico Mayor, former director general of UNESCO, wrote in 1989, "One of the most recent concepts to emerge in our time [is] that of the cultural heritage of mankind as a whole: through its realization that it shares a common destiny, mankind is finding out that it has a shared past, and the history of each country belongs to everyone" (quoted in Timken 1993:93). Historian Eric Foner (2002:xix) writes, "Who owns history? Everyone and no one—which is why the study of the past is a constantly evolving, never-ending journey of discovery."

I have written this book as an invitation for readers to join me on such a journey. I'd like to share some of the ambitions of historical archaeology and tell some of our stories. I've arranged the book into four sections, each of which has several short chapters. In the first section I introduce the goals of the field. One of the interesting things about the practice of archaeology is that, just like the archaeological record, it keeps adding on. Archaeologists don't really like to throw things away! We tend not to toss out our old goals or old questions, but we do refine them. In the second section I describe what historical archaeologists care about, including our questioning attitude, our topics, our evidence, and our ethics. In the third section I take you on a tour of excavations around the world. Archaeologists will often perform a "windshield survey" to get a sense of the landscape before getting out of the truck and actually looking for sites. Our version of a windshield in this book takes us through time and space to sample some of the work that historical archaeologists do. Public scholarship is the focus of the fourth section of this book, in keeping with my belief that scholars and researchers have a responsibility to develop and to participate in publicly meaningful work.

I'll be using terms and concepts that are best understood in the context of a case study. Rather than repeating myself, I'll refer you to places to go for further explanation when it seems helpful. Throughout the book, I've kept citations to a minimum. When I quote someone in the text I use the standard in-text social science style of citation already seen in this introduction. These works are in the References Cited section at the end of the book. Otherwise, you can find references for the work from which I have drawn, as well as additional publications that you'll find useful if you want to take your journey a little farther, in the Further Readings section.

No doubt that some of my colleagues would arrange this book a little differently, as we don't always see things the same way. (There is a joke we tell on ourselves: ask ten archaeologists a question and you'll get twelve answers.) As I've gathered my thoughts and impressions over my career of more than 25 years, I've watched historical archaeology grow and change remarkably. It's a journey I've never regretted.

SECTION ONE

What Are Our Ambitions?

CHAPTER 2

The Goals of Historical Archaeology

What we do about history matters. The often repeated saying that those who forget the lessons of history are doomed to repeat them has a lot of truth in it. But what are "the lessons of history"? The very attempt at definition furnishes ground for new conflicts. History is not a recipe book; past events are never replicated in the present in quite the same way. Historical events are infinitely variable and their interpretations are a constantly shifting process. There are no certainties to be found in the past.

—GERDA LERNER

It seems too simplistic, but archaeology's purpose today is to play a role in ending racism. Everything follows from this fact.

—ROBERT KELLY

How does historical archaeology become a method of *sankofa*, of asking questions about the past that relate to the present and help us toward a considered and intentional future? In this chapter I want to give you a broad overview of the current state of the field by categorizing our research goals; in the next section I get more specific about the kinds of questions and issues we tackle in our difficult and complex field. While I cannot claim that historical archaeology always fulfills its promise to be the kind of bridging past-to-future pursuit that it has the potential for, it is a rich and fascinating discipline.

As historian Gerda Lerner's remark reminds us, our response to history matters, and thus our approaches to it matter. Our goals must be broad and flexible and our willingness to learn must be vast. Archaeologist Robert Kelly researches time periods far earlier than the documented period; he works to understand the original ancient colonization of the Americas over ten thousand years ago. However, he states a goal that all archaeologists—whatever our specialties—can embrace, by highlighting the worthiness of all people and their past, however well or poorly known they may be. Kelly's stated purpose is anything but simplistic. I frequently consider how to connect what I do as an archaeologist with most of our everyday lives. Throughout this book I hope to stimulate thinking about how we use the past. How do we learn from it? How do we know that what we learn from it is accurate or true?

Historical archaeology in the United States is both a social science and one of the humanities, developing from both sides of its academic parentage in anthropology and history. Because of a common interest in American Indians, the fields of archaeology (the study of past cultures) and ethnography (the study of living cultures) developed together in departments of anthropology. Although historical archaeology's subject matter of life in documented time periods had more in common with American history, its methodology and ambitions eventually tied it more firmly to anthropology and anthropological archaeology. As one of the humanities (like history), historical archaeology seeks knowledge and understanding to gain insight into the human condition. As a social science (within the broader field of anthropology), historical archaeology's goals are to systematically investigate, describe, and explain human behavior. As part of anthropology, historical archaeology is becoming closely aligned with applied anthropology, which seeks to apply the lessons of research to real world issues.

Most historical archaeology concerns the past. But when did the past begin? Fifty years ago? Yesterday? This past-present boundary can be a problem for historical archaeologists because we have no neat dividing line. The methods and insights derived from working with material culture—the physical manifestations of what people do, think, and feel—are also applicable to the present. Therefore, archaeology doesn't recognize a strict or absolute time boundary for its subject matter.

Historical archaeology is practiced throughout the world. Roberta Gilchrist (2005:330) writes in an overview for the journal *World Archaeology*, "Today, historical archaeology dominates the practice of professional and contract archaeology across the globe, as urban development and historic building conservation yield massive archaeological data sets deriving from recent centuries." In the U.S. economy, for example, historical archaeologists work within the private sector in cultural resource management (CRM) firms and private foundations; the government sector in federal, tribal, state, and some local agencies; and the academic sector, although we are weakly represented in most colleges and universities.

Because so much historical archaeology is done as public archaeology that is funded or mandated by legal requirements, it is meant to provide public benefits. Public benefits involve not only knowledge and understanding gained through research, but also the use of sites and collections for such purposes as education and community cohesion. Historical archaeology's goals reach beyond professional research goals toward the needs of the many participants and publics who use and value it. I say more about the public face of the discipline throughout this book, in various examples and in the chapters on historical archaeology as public scholarship.

The field of historical archaeology necessarily crosses the borders between academic departments, drawing on many different disciplines for techniques, methods of analysis, theoretical perspectives, and application of research. Techniques, for example, include a full range of procedures, from geophysical prospecting for cellar holes with ground-penetrating radar to analyzing pollen and seeds to learn what was planted in a particular landscape. We adopt methods of analysis from such fields as material culture studies, ecology, bio-archaeology of human skeletal remains, and oral history. We borrow influential theoretical perspectives from a wide range of fields, including cultural anthropology, feminism, history, sociology, cultural studies, African American studies, and psychology. Applied research takes advantage of critical race studies, public history, and museum studies. I hope that as you read this book you'll think about the fields of study with which you are familiar and consider how they might intersect with a historical archaeological perspective that focuses on the material world.

Historical archaeology's goals have expanded as the discipline has grown. Broadly conceived, they fit under the rubrics of preserving and interpreting sites, supplementing and challenging the history we know through documents, reconstructing people's ways of life, improving archaeological methods, and understanding modernization and globalization. Connecting all of these goals is the thread of finding present-day meaning of the historical past and making the past meaningful and useful. Each of these goals presents enough compelling challenges to keep historical archaeologists and our colleagues in other fields working, arguing, and learning.

Other historical archaeologists might define our goals and purposes somewhat differently. I find it useful to think of our goals in this broad way first because they reflect the way that the field has developed and changed. Preservation and interpretation goals have been in place since the inception of the discipline and they continue to be important. The goal of adding to and challenging written history grew out of a realization that archaeology could reveal history that documents could not (rather than simply confirming recorded history), and this goal is most closely related to historical archaeology as history. In contrast, reconstructing lifeways is more closely related to historical archaeology as anthropology and specifically as ethnography (the study of living people). This goal grew out of the ambition of the field to be accepted as part of a historically oriented anthropology.

Improving more general archaeological methods is no longer a primary motivator for the field, although it remains important. It was particularly prevalent in the early decades when it was not yet clear that archaeology of the recent past could contribute new or unique information. Many archaeologists wanted to use the historic period as a sort of laboratory where certain knowledge and conditions could be held constant so that methods could be tested or developed. Although no longer seen as a necessary "excuse" for historic period research, clarifying and critiquing methods and concepts remains a worthwhile goal.

The goal of understanding modernization and globalization is a logical outgrowth of defining the field's scope as the half millennium since European global exploration. This particular goal inspires many of the topics I discuss in chapters 9 and 10.

The thread that ties all of our goals together might be thought of as the relevance of the archaeological past: What does it mean? What value does it have? How can we use it to learn and create a better present and future? How is it a path of *sankofa*, whereby we can connect past and future?

CHAPTER 3

Preserving and Interpreting Sites

Let us, while waiting for new monuments, preserve the ancient monuments.
—VICTOR HUGO

Historical archaeology **often** is used to document architectural and landscape details for the management of public lands and for public interpretation at monuments and parks. Because the field had its professional beginnings in the context of the preservation movement, I want to take a quick look at its development.

During the latter half of the 19th century, the modern preservation movement in the United States got started with the preservation of George Washington's home in northern Virginia by the Mount Vernon Ladies Association. Preservation in the East focused on buildings associated with the founding fathers and other patriotic history. On the other side of the continent, 19th-century preservation efforts took a somewhat different focus, although they were no less important to creating a sense of national identity. There was great interest in protecting archaeological sites, particularly in the Southwest. In 1892 President Benjamin Harrison created the first national archaeological reservation at Casa Grande Ruins in Arizona. Other efforts to protect specific and spectacular resources such as Mesa Verde in Colorado and Chaco Canyon in New Mexico led to important federal legislation. The Antiquities Act, passed in 1906, established the basic preservation policies of the United States federal government. Francis McManamon, the chief archaeologist of the National Park Service, describes the impact of the act on the development of archaeology as a profession:

> The Antiquities Act established the requirement of professionalism and a scientific approach for any…investigation of archaeological resources on public

lands. By so doing, the government of the United States endorsed the young discipline of archaeology and the careful examination and recording of archaeological sites that its leaders were then working to establish as a basis for their practice. (1996:18)

One of the provisions of the Antiquities Act is to grant the president the means to establish national monuments on federal land. Among the first 17 established by Teddy Roosevelt were six archaeological properties, including the Tumacacori Mission site in Arizona (designated in 1908), where historical archaeologists began excavating just a few decades later in a rush of mission archaeology that started during the 1930s.

The Antiquities Act was the foundation for later acts—the Historic Sites Act of 1935 and the National Historic Preservation Act of 1966—both of which extended the policies to other kinds of historic properties. Section 1 of the Historic Sites Act of 1935 states: "It is hereby declared that it is a national policy to preserve for public use historic sites, buildings, and objects of national significance for the inspiration and benefit of the people of the United States." Congress also took that inspirational intent seriously when it passed the National Historic Preservation Act (NHPA) in 1966. This law established the National Register of Historic Places and the criteria for listing significant historic places as worthy of preservation. Eventually the NHPA stimulated the growth of historical archaeology through its requirements for survey for historic properties from all time periods. The sheer volume of historical archaeology projects undertaken in the United States increased dramatically with this legislation and its regulations.

In the 1930s archaeologists embarked on major projects at such widely different places as Jamestown in Virginia and La Purisima Mission in California. Such large-scale excavations in historical archaeology embedded the practice firmly in the realm of public interpretation. Early in the history of such work, it was usually architects rather than archaeologists who interpreted the structural remains. Archaeologists, however, eventually managed to gain control of the discipline and their work has provided the specifications for many accurate reconstructions that are tourist attractions.

For example, extensive archaeology and documentary research in archives in France provided the information needed to accurately reconstruct a portion of the Fortress of Louisbourg on Cape Breton Island in Nova Scotia, Canada. The story of Louisbourg is tied to cod fishing, to European power struggles, and, more recently, to economic development needs. Europe's voyages of discovery had led to the rich fishing and whaling grounds off the eastern coast of North America. During the 1500s and 1600s, fishermen from France, England, Spain, and Portugal exploited the cod fisheries in the summers and sailed home for the winter without establishing substantial settlements. European wars threatened France's hold on North America and when the Treaty of Utrecht was signed in 1713 to end the War of the Spanish Succession, France lost both Acadia and Newfoundland to England. As a result, France established Louisbourg to claim a strategic foothold in the New World. In 1713 about 150 people established the town for cod fishing and trading. Work on the fortifications began a few years later. The ice-free harbor was well situated for important fishing grounds and trade routes with France, Canada, and the West Indies.

Peace between France and England lasted just a few decades. The Seven Years' War (also known as the French and Indian War) put these countries back on the battlefield. After the British captured Louisbourg they deported the French inhabitants to France and destroyed the fortifications in 1760. Two hundred years later, the Canadian government embarked on a reconstruction effort both to provide work for unemployed coal miners and to create a destination for visitors to learn about life in 18th-century New France. Archaeologists continue to investigate the many archaeological sites surrounding the reconstruction to learn about the daily lives of townspeople and soldiers.

There are quite a few reconstructions of forts and missions based on archaeology, although you won't necessarily learn about the research process or underlying evidence when visiting these places. For example, in the late 1940s and early 1950s the archaeologist J. C. Harrington excavated Fort Necessity in western Pennsylvania. This fort was the 1754 scene of the pivotal conflict between England and France that opened the French and Indian War (the colonial troops commanded by 22-year-old Colonel George Washington were defeated.) Archaeology revealed that long-held assumptions about the fort's precise location, size, and shape were wrong. Excavation identified the stockade and outer entrenchments and permitted an accurate reconstruction as a circular fort, which is managed by the National Park Service.

There are many more examples of reconstructions based on archaeological data, including an amazing number of forts (such as Fort Stanwix in New York, Fort Michilimackinac in Michigan, Bent's Old Fort in Colorado, Fort Union Trading Post in North Dakota, Arkansas Post in Arkansas, Fort Larned and Fort Scott in Kansas, Fort Vancouver and Whitman Mission in Washington, and Fort Ross in California). Several of the reconstructed buildings at the fur trading post of Grand Portage National Monument in northeastern Minnesota are based on excavations done in the 1930s, which were funded by the Civilian Conservation Corps through the United States Indian Service during the Depression. The Grand Portage Ojibwe Indian Reservation was involved in this effort to create jobs and tourism.

Archaeology has suited such government jobs programs because it requires a relatively large labor force with a range of skill levels. Even today, many individuals who work on archaeological projects are not professional archaeologists and may have no intention of following that career path. Many people want a little taste of excavation or laboratory work and volunteer, take field schools, or work temporarily on an archaeology project. For many others, it is a lifelong hobby.

Figure 1. In some cases archaeologically based reconstructions are not fully built. Benjamin Franklin's house is represented by a "ghost structure" at Independence National Historical Park. (*Photo by author*)

Across the globe historical archaeology also serves to uncover and interpret history through heritage tourism. There are, for example, quite a few sites you can visit to see the results of archaeology in Sydney and throughout New South Wales and other parts of Australia. In Tasmania you can visit the site of the famous penal colony of Port Arthur, as well as the Ross Female Factory Site where female convicts were incarcerated in the 1840s and 1850s. You can visit La Maison des Esclaves in Senegal and Elmina and Cape Coast in Ghana. These slave "castles" and dungeons housed captives before they were loaded on the ships for the Middle Passage during the transatlantic slave trade. At Red Bay in Labrador, Canada, Parks Canada provides a compelling worth-the-trip interpretation of the remains of a 16th-century Basque whaling port including onshore whaling stations and sunken galleons and other craft. I am particularly fond of the site of L'Anse aux Meadows in Newfoundland (even though I gave in and bought mittens during my chilly August visit). Here, Parks Canada preserves the archaeological site of this well-known Viking settlement. Nearby they have reconstructed Norse buildings and some other features on the landscape so that visitors don't have to rely wholly on either their imagination or the fine museum exhibits to get a sense of the place a thousand years ago.

Historical archaeologists continue to excavate sites for the purposes of accurate visitor interpretation. Sometimes reconstructions are substantial and fully built. Other structures may simply suggest their former selves. Figure 1 shows a "ghost structure" that represents Benjamin Franklin's house in Philadelphia, Pennsylvania, in Independence National Historical Park. This type of reconstruction conveys a sense of how partial our knowledge is about an above-ground building based on below-ground evidence. I'll return to the possibilities and responsibilities of presenting the past as we go along and in the section on public scholarship, especially in chapter 25, on public memory and public places.

CHAPTER 4

Rewriting Documentary History

From time to time historians need to be shocked.

—PETER BURKE

Archaeology supplements our knowledge about the past in the sense that it might fill in gaps created by biased and incomplete records. Sometimes archaeologists justify our interest in the recent past because the poor, disenfranchised, or illiterate tend not to appear in documentation. Or, when they do, the available information is distorted and incomplete. Therefore archaeology may be the primary source of information about many people's lives. Because archaeological and documentary evidence are completely different types of evidence, it is not a straightforward matter to cobble them together to create a comprehensive picture of the past.

Historical archaeologists use documents and historic methods, but they use them in conjunction with material culture and often challenge history derived from documents by providing alternative questions and interpretations. An archaeological approach may raise questions not otherwise asked. Sometimes these questions are spurred by inhabitants of the specific places where archaeologists happen to find themselves working. Such place-based investigation can stimulate researchers to think beyond accepted historical interpretation or to revisit alternative histories.

In 1983 an accidental grass fire exposed the surface of Little Bighorn Battlefield in eastern Montana, providing an opportunity to examine the ground surface and to conduct archaeological investigations. This battle is one of the most famous of the many conflicts over control of land and life in the American West. On June 25, 1876, the Seventh U.S. Cavalry, led by Lieutenant Colonel George Armstrong Custer, engaged the Sioux and Cheyenne tribes in a battle that was part of the United States government's military campaign against the tribes, who refused to live within the boundaries of the Great Sioux Reservation and were instead struggling to continue their traditional way of life. Because none of the Seventh Cavalry combatants survived, there were no eyewitness accounts from Euro-Americans. Professional historians tended to discount the accounts of the Native Americans.

The researchers of this site created innovative archaeological methods that involved using modern firearm identification procedures. Their work has changed the way that battlefield archaeology is done and has opened up a whole new set of questions and methods for military history. Specific unanswered questions concerned where the participants of the battle took up positions and how they moved about the field. The archaeologists used excavation and geophysical techniques, including the use of metal detectors, to translate the patterns of recovered artifacts into a reconstruction of how the combatants fought. Some historians had long held that the extensive Native American testimony was not accurate. Archaeological discoveries challenged historical details and versions of the battle that had long been accepted by non–Native American historians. Findings support the idea that the Native American battle accounts are more accurate than those of the soldiers who buried the dead.

There are other examples as well of archaeology supporting "alternative" history and challenging an accepted perspective. Often, oral history and archaeology are mutually supportive in providing data and perspectives that contribute to a more accurate history in which biases and the politics of knowledge are acknowledged. However, there are also cases in which oral tradition is proven wrong. An example comes from Newport, Rhode Island. The Newport Tower, also called the Viking Tower or the Mystery Tower, is a stone structure surrounded with hopeful legends about pre-Columbian explorers. However, in the 1940s historical archaeologists discovered artifacts and other evidence that reliably date the tower's construction to sometime around the 1650s. (Another clue is provided by Rhode Island's governor from that time, whose will refers to his "stone windmill.") Of course physical evidence does not necessarily convince those who really want to believe something exotic. Unfortunately, it is not all that unusual for such evidence to be ignored in favor of more fanciful stories.

In a similar way, some finds challenge commonly "known" history and raise questions that might change our popular ways of thinking about the past. In 1865 the steamboat *Bertrand*, bound from St. Louis for the newly discovered goldfields of Montana, sank in the Missouri River north of Omaha, Nebraska.

Archaeologists completely excavated the vessel's hull in 1969, recovering tools, clothing, food, and equipment that were in remarkably good condition because they had been preserved in the oxygen-free underwater environment. The objects bound for the mining towns are not quite what we might expect to find on the raucous 19th-century American frontier. In addition to necessities, there were olive oil and mustard from France, bottled tamarinds and a variety of canned fruits, several varieties of alcoholic bitters, powdered canned lemonade, and brandied cherries. Such an inventory challenges some Hollywood-inspired assumptions about roughing it on the frontier and also provides an important resource for researchers of frontier life and consumer culture.

One more example comes from early industry. Saugus Iron Works, located just ten miles north of Boston, Massachusetts, was the site of the first successful ironworks in the English colonies. Operating from 1646 to 1668, the industrial complex produced cast- and wrought-iron products. The general location of the complex was clearly marked on the landscape by the very large slag pile produced by the industrial operations. During the late 1940s and early 1950s excavations uncovered the holding ponds and canal, the wheel pit, half of the blast furnace waterwheel, and thousands of artifacts. Because there was scant documentary evidence of this site, researchers had previously relied upon what was known about other such operations for interpreting the building foundations and water power features. The perfectly reasonable working assumption was that this was an ordinary low-technology furnace. One particular archaeological discovery challenged that assumption. The clue was a piece of iron about 8 to 10 inches long, 3 inches wide, and half an inch thick, partially cut through lengthwise leaving several strips connected at one end. The presence of this artifact indicated that Saugus Iron Works had a slitting mill, which rolled iron bars and then could slit them into smaller strips mainly used for nails. This level of technological sophistication was present only at about a dozen ironworks in the world in the mid-17th century, so it was certainly a surprise to find it in Massachusetts.

I've chosen these very different examples to illustrate some ways in which material evidence challenges, corrects, or refines what we think we know about the past. We'll come across some more examples as we go along, particularly in the case study of Jamestown in chapter 15.

CHAPTER 5

Reconstructing Ways of Life

People always seemed to know half of history, and to get it confused with the other half.

—JANE HADDAM

We can think about historical archaeology's goal to reconstruct ways of life as historical anthropology, which describes past lifeways in terms of foodways, settlement patterns, domestic life, economic relationships, social structures, and worldviews. The reconstruction of past cultures and lifeways intersects with anthropologists' and historians' explanations of regional and global processes such as colonialism, capitalism, and slavery and contributes to our understandings of the lives of a full range of people in past societies.

Of particular interest to an archaeology of the modern world is the experience of migration, as people moved in large numbers to the Americas, Australia, and other colonies. The new governments often sought to attract settlers. For example, Canada's free homestead land was meant to entice immigrants to settle the West. In response, thousands of Doukhobors fled Tsarist persecution in Russia in 1899 and established several colonies. Archaeologists investigating their settlement of Kirilovka in Saskatchewan were looking for evidence of the specific belief-based behavior that set them apart as a distinct cultural group in Canadian society.

The sect originated as a reformation movement against the Russian Orthodox Church in the 18th century. Several points are key to their philosophy: a belief in a divine spark in every living thing and therefore the equality of all life, rejection of worldly government (including structured religious institutions), and salvation through daily practice of faith. While in Siberia, the sect split into factions, one of which was led by Peter Verigin who, in his role as a nearly divine leader, prescribed specific behaviors of communalism, pacifism, vegetarianism, and the avoidance of alcohol and tobacco.

The archaeological evidence contradicts daily adherence to the rules imposed by Verigin. In spite of a rule against the use of intoxicants, the unmistakable material remains of wine, whiskey, gin, and beer bottles indicate that alcohol was consumed on-site. Archaeological remains of butchered beef, poultry, and rabbit were found along with the bones of officially sanctioned fish. Clearly, some households simply chose not to obey the prohibitions, although they may have been silent about their choices. At another Doukhobor site, descendants (no longer vegetarians) found the remains of butchered bone somewhat upsetting because they are proud of their ancestors' convictions. One present-day Doukhobor told of non-Doukhobor men who worked for her grandparents and who threatened to leave if they were not fed meat. Therefore, this volunteer and descendant proposed the possible explanation that the archaeological evidence was the result of the workers being supplied with butchered meat rather than her grandparents' breaking religious prohibitions.

The interpretation of communal and egalitarian values in this instance is somewhat less straightforward, but the evidence does not support the ideal of a community where every family lives alike. Through analyzing household ceramics, archaeologists found family rather than communal dining and a great deal of variety and inequality among households. Individual families appear to have been acquiring consumer goods quite separately from their neighbors.

The Doukhobor archaeology raises questions about ways of life and the connection of behavior to belief. It is too simplistic (and cynical) to use the archaeological evidence to dismiss the sincerity of religious belief. Practices imposed on a group to distinguish a faction, as Verigin appears to have done, may have little lasting effect if they are not fully embedded in culture. Many utopian communities find it difficult or impossible to maintain an idealized way of life within the turbulence of the surrounding world. As archaeologist Stacy Kozakavich (2006:130), who worked at Kirilovka, remarks, "During their many migrations, Doukhobors carried visions of a perfect society attainable through the daily practice of their religion. They maintained this ideal more in mind and philosophy than in reality, as specific circumstances rarely fostered the realization of such Utopian aspirations."

Another example of European immigrants in western North America concerns contact between Native people and Russian colonists and the ways of life each developed in this radically new era. The Russians began to advance their eastern frontier across Siberia in the late 16th and early 17th centuries to capitalize on furs, first encountering Native Alaskans in 1741. Russians followed their military conquest with forced labor and mandatory tribute. It was a very different approach to the fur "trade" than that taken by the French and English in their colonies, because it scarcely qualified as a trading relationship. Even after 1840, the quantity of trade goods other than glass beads at Alaskan sites was quite limited, supplying a useful caution against the usual archaeological assumption that the quantity of goods is a measure of the intensity of contact.

Russia annexed Alaska and founded the Russian-American Company in 1799 to administer the territory until the United States purchased it in 1867. From 1828 to 1867, they established dozens of outposts, including missions, in Alaska and also in the Kurile Islands north of Japan. The Russians settled Fort Ross in California from 1812 to 1841 and established a brief occupation in Hawaii at Fort Elisabeth on Kaua'i from 1816 to 1817.

The Russians transported some Aleut far from their homes in Alaska to various locations, including Fort Ross, which is north of San Francisco. Excavations at and around the fort provide opportunity to examine a multiethnic settlement and ask questions about labor division, social organization, and gender roles. Such research allows us to compare the settlements of different colonial powers and the strategies of different Native groups in response. The workforce consisted of Alaskan men and their families and Native California groups, including Kashaya Pomo, Southern Pomo, and Coastal Miwok men and women. Outside of the fort's palisade walls was the Alaska Native Village Site, with a complex blend of Alaskan, Californian, and Russian material culture. Native American workers did not buy European goods, but acquired them as discarded items. They recycled materials such as nails and ceramic and glass sherds, transforming them into objects that were useful in the Native American context and within a complex set of Native cultural strategies to retain cultural identity and to cope with displacement and forced labor.

Here we've taken a look at some Russians fleeing oppression and some other Russians leaving home in search of profits to be gained from fur. Native peoples' lives also were deeply affected by both the settlement of foreigners and the exploitation of natural resources. There are many examples of people's lives changing drastically in the last several centuries. Many of the case studies in section 3 provide further examples of such far-reaching change.

CHAPTER 6

Improving Archaeological Methods

What is standing in the way of further scientific discovery is not our igno-
rance but the illusion of knowledge.

—LAURA NADER

nthropologist Laura Nader's observation is a reminder of the need
to continually improve our research concepts and methods. Archaeologists have used remains of the historic period as a laboratory for more general
archaeological science to be perfected through ethnoarchaeology (archaeological study of living people and their material world) and material culture
studies (interdisciplinary study of objects through archaeology, history, folklore, anthropology, and the history of science and technology). Such work
covers a range of topics. Some archaeologists have tested seriation (techni-
cally, putting things in a series) as a relative dating method that depends on
the gradual change in fashion from one style to another. Others try to identify predictable ways that people with different cultural backgrounds throw
out their trash (refuse is, after all, much of what archaeologists have to work
with). Still others want to understand the ways that artifacts and other material culture marks the status (high or low) of individuals or groups. In addition, observing and predicting the effects of flooding, erosion, plowing, and
other natural or cultural processes upon the archaeological record can help
decode the way that sites are formed. By undertaking such work, some historical archaeologists continue to develop methods that will further the general
techniques and methods of archaeology.

The study of historic period burial practices has provided some perspective on assumed links between an individual's status and the elaboration of
his or her burial. The Weir cemetery in northern Virginia, dating from the
1830s to 1907, was a very small family cemetery excavated at the request of

family members because a housing development was about to surround it and they wanted the burials moved closer to the original family home. I worked with Kim Lanphear and Douglas Owsley to analyze this site, which we excavated with a crew of volunteers, including one descendant who operated the backhoe. We identified four styles of burial among the 24 graves. These styles track four different periods, reflecting not status but the appearance, peak, and decline of the Victorian-era phenomenon known as the "beautification of death." During the 19th century, there was a marked increase in the expense and ritual associated with death, demonstrated by mourning clothing, adornment of the home of the deceased with funeral crepe and wreaths, erection of elaborate grave markers, and decorative arts commemorating death. Such visual display mirrored the emotional intensity of Romanticism and the sentimentality associated with death.

We can think about this elaboration phenomenon as an example of a cyclical process of display that has been termed the "invisible-ink strategy." In general terms, a group that uses this common nonverbal strategy cultivates certain kinds of knowledge, such as proper burial custom, to clearly mark group membership or status. Then, members change the requisite knowledge and behavior often enough to identify and exclude outsiders. In this way elites, for example, seek to guard their symbols of privilege by preventing lower-class emulation from becoming a threat to elite identity.

We all can probably think of other examples of fashion being used to identify those "in the know." We do this frequently to identify members of our in-groups, sometimes in obvious ways: Who owns and knows how to use the latest digital music technology? Who is behind the fashion curve in their clothing or hairstyle and what does that mean for how we judge them? Sometimes the strategies are less obvious than those demonstrated by technological or fashion ownership and know-how, but seeing how they work in the past can help identify how they work in the present, and vice versa.

Among the Weir graves, the elaboration of the burials depends on when they were buried in the cycle of display. We assigned dates to burials mainly through their headstones, but also through the availability of coffin handles and other hardware found in trade catalogs. There was little elaboration before the rise of the idea, followed by expensive grave goods at its peak, and then post-Victorian understatement when elite fashion changed. The earliest burials received almost no decoration. In the second set of burials coffins were more decorated, marking the beginning of the cycle of elaboration. Praying angels depicted on some coffin handles are the most obvious example of Victorian influence. In the third set most burials showed many decorative elements, but by the final period such elaboration had ceased. The Weir family didn't change in social status through this period, although their financial status declined due to the loss of their slaves. Without taking into account the invisible-ink strategy and attitudes about death provided by historical context, we could have read the cemetery as a testament to the rise and fall of social status.

Understanding some of the language of material culture as we can decode it in the historic period with the benefit of documents and explicit cultural context can help us understand other options for decoding material culture in the past where we don't understand the culture quite so well. The rise and eventual fall of the idealized beautification of death points up the fallacy of assuming a direct relationship between apparently rich burial goods and high social status. This is particularly true since elite cycles of display are not restricted to the historic period. This observation may seem counterintuitive, particularly if we assume that wealth and elite class membership is always communicated in the same way.

Historical archaeological studies that contribute to general archaeological method often take the form of cautionary tales to warn colleagues about unexpected complexity in the archaeological record. By providing test cases for theory building, they allow archaeologists to test assumptions and to refine their logic by broadening the range of factors that must be considered in interpreting material remains. In the case of applying lessons from the Weir family cemetery to undocumented cemeteries, the caution is to refrain from automatically associating more costly burial goods with elite status of the buried individuals.

CHAPTER 7

Understanding Modernization and Globalization

The purpose of anthropology is to make the world safe for human differences.
—RUTH BENEDICT

As historical archaeologists were defining and stabilizing the profession in the 1960s—establishing professional organizations and journals—there were high hopes for its potential as a kind of laboratory for anthropology, particularly concerning processes such as colonization and acculturation (culture change brought about through cultural contact). Many practitioners see the continued potential for investigating such processes, although anthropological models have gotten much more complex. Studying colonization, for example, requires that we study power, domination, and resistance on many levels. Acculturation is a complex economic, political, and symbolic process. I look more closely at colonialism and acculturation in chapter 10 and at dominant ideology and resistance in chapter 12. Understanding modernization and globalization is a goal that is firmly embedded in our understanding of historical archaeology as a way to understand the development of the modern world.

Historical archaeologists take a long-term view on globalization, considering the development of the global world system over the past 500 years. This view contrasts with a more familiar definition of globalization as a very recent and rapidly moving set of economic and social changes occurring worldwide since the collapse of the Soviet Union. Archaeology tells us something important about these earlier globalizations, namely that people were moving, in large numbers and for a variety of reasons. Wars, persecution, and economic collapse at home, as well as opportunities abroad, motivated many people to move. Sometimes they were welcome in their new lands, but sometimes they faced discrimination. Regardless, they left indelible marks on the land and in society.

Consider the overseas Chinese. In the mid-19th century, news of gold discoveries in California lured droves of fortune seekers, from across the country (those "Forty-Niners") and across the ocean. Chinese men came in search of both economic and social freedom, escaping difficult times at home fueled by the British Opium War (1839–1842) and the Tai Ping Rebellion (1851–1864). Often their dream was to earn money with which to return home and buy land in their home villages in order to support their extended family. During the construction of the transcontinental railroad, Chinese laborers came to North America as laborers to build the railroad. In addition to California, they followed opportunities across the West, moving to Nevada, Arizona, New Mexico, Oregon, Washington, and Idaho. Chinese emigrants also migrated to Peru, Australia, New Zealand, and Southeast Asia. Archaeologist Julia Costello summarizes:

> After the railroad was completed, and the gold fields played out, Chinese spread to other industries, predominantly agriculture, fishing, and manufacturing. Chinatowns grew as retail and cultural centers to support this working population. In 1880, the Chinese in California reached a population height of over 75,000. In 1882, the Chinese Exclusion Act was passed…and the flow of Chinese diminished markedly.… Anti-Chinese sentiment enflamed many communities. (2004:15)

Archaeology of the overseas Chinese in America tells of stereotypes, prejudice, and a lost heritage of globalization that can be recovered. In the 19th-century climate of violent prejudice, the Chinese often found themselves illogically blamed for their "evil influence." Contemporary newspapers also complained about illegal Chinese gambling houses and opium use. Opium was legal in the United States until 1909; only European Americans could import it and they sold it to the Chinese. Many people used it as a social drug, much like many of us use tobacco or alcohol today. Gambling as recreation, of course, was popular and widespread among European Americans as well as the Chinese. The actual "evil influence" turns out to be the pernicious judgmental stereotypes that have haunted people of Chinese descent.

An example of a uniquely Chinese site type marking global migrations is the terraced landscape garden. Jeffrey Fee describes some of these in the remote Salmon River drainage in central Idaho near the mining town of Warren. Gold was discovered in 1862 near the Salmon River and until the rich pay dirt was depleted, Chinese were not allowed to stake claims. Only after 1869 were Chinese miners allowed to lease and rework abandoned claims. Chinese became the majority ethnic group in this area from about 1870 until the turn of the century, working not only as miners but also in support businesses in the town and as farmers.

The town of Warren is at 6000 feet elevation; Chinese gold miners built terrace gardens at elevations ranging from 3200 to 4700 feet. The miner-farmers irrigated the gardens from the same ditches that they constructed for mining their claims. They built extensive gardens as commercial ventures to supply themselves and the population of the Warren mining district with fresh fruits and vegetables. A few of Fee's (1993:94) concluding words remind us of the ways that global phenomena are etched on the landscape as well as under the soil: "The terrace gardens remain quiet and clothed in natural vegetation yet visibly carved into those Salmon River mountains. Here we have a glimpse of China in the backcountry of Idaho; a constant reminder of Asian contributions on American soil."

It is impossible to research the development of the modern world without some perspective on global population movements and far-flung economic connections. Many of the case studies in our windshield survey speak to globalization in some way. In particular we see global connections in many diaspora communities. Our look at the archaeology of the African diaspora is scattered throughout, but see especially chapters 20 and 27. We'll investigate a bit of the Irish diaspora in chapter 19 on Australia, in chapter 22 on the inner-city working class, and in chapter 29 on civic renewal and restorative justice.

SECTION TWO

What Do We Care About?

CHAPTER 8

A Questioning Attitude

Questioning is thought, giving rise to anguish and doubt, while answering is a kind of cessation of thought, bringing confidence and certainty. Questioning, in other words, is thought which provokes more thought.

— ADONIS ('ALI AHMAD SA'ID)

I am continually astonished at the richness of the past that archaeology reveals. I think about the Harris Poll finding that Americans believe archaeology is important because it can help us improve the future and understand the modern world. I agree. I also know that it is easier said than done to understand the present using examples of the past. We want to see where we came from, to understand how we got here. Our goals as historical archaeologists complement and reinforce each other to help along that path. Reconstructing past ways of life can also become part of the story at a historic park; improving our methods and concepts can help us ask more sophisticated questions about past and present globalization. Now I want to turn to the way we ask questions.

I've given a general idea of how historical archaeology is defined and what we aim to do. I need to be a little more specific about how we connect with other types of archaeology and how that is changing. Our time period depends on the boundaries of our evidence and questions. If the availability of both documentary and material sources—and hence a common range of evidence—is thought of as the defining factor, then historical archaeology encompasses all "text-aided" archaeology and has a domain as deep as that of written language. In fact, in the early 18th century "historical archaeology" (although it was not called that) was the sort of work carried out at Herculaneum and Pompeii, Roman towns famous for their extraordinary preservation in the wake of the Mount Vesuvius eruption of A.D. 79.

Because such excavations were a source of ancient texts as well as artifacts, they served at the time to bridge the familiar study of historical documents and the unfamiliar study of artifacts. Before archaeology could develop further, scholars needed to get beyond the restrictive (and, I might add, remarkably persistent) assumption that without written documents there could be no historical knowledge.

Traditionally, archaeology of the ancient Western world is done by classicists and is termed classical archaeology. Biblical archaeology investigates the Judeo-Christian scriptures as historical texts and is done by Biblical archaeologists. Those who identify themselves as "historical archaeologists" usually define their discipline differently, with a focus on the modern world. In this case, the boundaries are determined by the globalizing effect of European exploration and colonization. The field covers approximately the last 500 years.

This latter definition is more manageable and especially applicable to Europe's colonies. I adopt it for this book, but it is certainly imperfect. I feel it's important to point out one of the difficulties that arises with this European-focused definition. As I've mentioned, historical archaeology in the United States has developed in the context of its parent disciplines of history and anthropology, including "prehistoric" archaeology, which takes as its subject indigenous populations in the Americas before the arrival of Europeans and subsequent contact between these peoples. The long-standing divisions between precontact and historic archaeology, particularly when the subject is intercultural contact, can work against some kinds of questions. That division, for example, can make it difficult to understand the long, dynamic history of Native peoples as a continuum everywhere there was colonization. It is certainly the case that things changed drastically as Europeans spread across Australia and the Americas, taking Africans with them. Therefore, the time frame is not illogical from the viewpoint of the modern world, but we should try to be aware of the biases that can creep into our analyses as a result. Specifically, if you are European American, as I am, it is far too easy to adopt the deeply flawed, yet common, attitude that "it's all about us." It is difficult to wrest archaeology away from a white-centered perspective, although it is clearly possible, as demonstrated especially by recent approaches to the archaeology of the African diaspora.

In some cases, the boundary between "prehistoric" and historic archaeologies are blurring, brought on by the recognition that Europeans did not bring history to the worlds that were completely new to them: written language and especially printing (among other things), yes, but not history. Historical change is a constant for all societies, and indigenous people have borne the brunt of an 18th-century Enlightenment perspective that branded cultural change in Native populations as the equivalent of cultural disintegration. That is, anthropologists and archaeologists saw change in Native societies as unnatural and leading to some sort of "inauthentic" culture.

About this tendency, anthropologist Marshall Sahlins (1999:ii) has observed, "Certain illusions born of the Western self-consciousness of civilization have thus proved not too enlightening." Sahlins is criticizing the rigid models and expectations that have passed for universal truth, even though they are very much a product of Western thinking, bound within that specific social and cultural context. He continues: "Anthropology needs to free itself from sexism, positivism, geneticism, utilitarianism, and many other such dogmas of the common average native Western folklore posing as universal understandings of the human condition." His words recall the poet Adonis's observation I quote at the beginning of this chapter. Allowing ourselves to question allows us to think and to learn. Anguish (well, at least some discomfort) and doubt are a necessary part of the process.

Sahlins' critique has emerged from his willingness to learn from past mistakes and current evidence and thereby to move forward (there's the concept of *sankofa* again). I find such willingness to be an essential feature of any historical archaeology that truly seeks to question and learn.

I began this chapter with a quote from the poet Adonis because I appreciate his observations about questioning, answering, and the relationship among these, our thought processes, and our states of mind. I find it exhilarating to think about our quest for knowledge and understanding as a continual journey, never ending and full of surprises, twists, and serendipitous discovery. Is it always comfortable to challenge what I thought I knew? No. But it is difficult to grow—either personally or as a scholarly discipline—without some degree of discomfort. As I described earlier, historical archaeology is both a humanity and a social science. It relies on both art and science and a willingness to question and learn relentlessly. Working with our wide range of evidence demonstrates the ambiguity inherent in human expression. I am referring not only to material culture but also to words on paper, the meaning of which is rarely clear or final.

If historical archaeologists want our work to have broad meaning, then we have to keep broad questions in mind. For example, a question about the past that leads to questions about the present and future might be: how have people struggled with change? The types of change can be occurring in culture, economy, politics, religion, science, gender, industry, social structure, language, technology, media, or otherwise. We see change in the world around us constantly, even in simple things like the ways immigration of people from other places affects the food that is available in our communities or the ways that land and space are used. Such changes in the past are often recorded in the archaeological record (particularly in the era before landfills).

If we want our work to become a method of *sankofa*, then we need to be willing to learn. If the accepted history is silent about certain parts of the past (because the same topics are taboo in the present), how can historical archaeology identify the silences? We must actively seek out those culturally enforced silences, rather than celebrating what's culturally sanctioned. We should challenge ourselves: How do we identify and find evidence for the ugly parts of our history, such as racism, homophobia, and domestic violence? How do we begin to provide a language for the unspoken parts of culture, such as sexuality, profit, complicity, and corruption? How can we separate our own ethical judgments from contemporary cultural perspectives and attitudes?

Currently, many historical archaeologists define their major research issues in terms of the formation and maintenance of separations based on race, ethnicity, class, or gender. Such separations occur in all time periods and many settings. Certainly differences among groups are persistent and the history of conflict matters, particularly when injustice, prejudice, and inequality persist. However, there are some advantages to recasting "lines that divide" into "struggles that unite." I recognize that either extreme—focusing only on conflict or only on common ground—can be problematic and even misleading. I'll return to some of these ideas in section 4, which focuses on public scholarship.

Historical archaeology is often influenced directly by trends in the disciplines of both history and anthropology. These parent fields also influence and borrow from each other. The pendulum swings in each between global and local research. In their compelling look at trends in their field, historians Joyce Appleby, Lynne Hunt, and Margaret Jacob write of historians becoming a little gun-shy of the big issues:

> Contemporary historians have retreated to smaller questions—not why capitalism triumphed in the West, but what happened to displaced weavers when mechanization came to Gloucestershire. Late-twentieth-century historians find a uniqueness in the complexity of events which mocks the earlier mimicry of the scientific model of uniform truths. (1995:303)

Still, many historical archaeologists, inspired by both historians' and anthropologists' once and future global ambitions, are looking outward toward global issues, while keeping in mind that archaeology is done one site at a time. Charles Orser proposes that historical archaeologists frame their questions in a way that's mindful of the "haunts" of the developing modern world—that is, those legacies of the past which continue to affect us. These haunts of colonialism, Eurocentrism, capitalism, and modernity cannot be truly separated and all are fully loaded terms, but the latter haunt is particularly packed with further implications. Decades ago journalist Walter Lippmann listed the "acids of modernity" as industrialism, urbanism, science, secularism, and internationalism. Sociologist Anthony Giddens identifies the institutional aspects of modernity as capitalism, industrialism, surveillance, and military power. However we define the "haunts" that need to be present in our work—and I would argue that gender ideology, literacy, religious institutions, and all manifestations of spiritual heritage should be among them—the global aspirations of the field are currently quite clear.

Anthropologist Laura Nader celebrates the transformation of anthropology at the turn of the millennium and calls this a time for "new syntheses and renewed civic engagement" (2001:609). Nader has confidence in the discipline's ability to thrive and make real contributions in the modern world. It's a confidence shared by historical archaeologists. She writes:

> The anthropological perspective, disrespectful as it is of boundaries and cherished truths, continues to permeate the social sciences and the humanities, other disciplines, intelligent lay people, people in high places.... [I]t is the anthropological perspective that ... sees what others often do not see, that makes connections that are not made elsewhere, that questions assumptions and exoticizes behavior that is normalized, that asks plain questions like, "What's going on around here?" (2001:610)

What indeed? How does historical archaeology contribute? Why are we interested in knowing about cultural expression through artifacts? In an age of global consumerism, it is reasonable to be interested in how people choose and use things, how they impart meaning to them, and how they accept or reject them. In an age of imperial disintegration and renegotiated economic and political relationships, it is reasonable to ask how groups of individuals have redefined themselves and their societies, how they have acted collectively to achieve their goals, and how, through material culture, they have shaped, expressed, hidden, and celebrated their identities.

CHAPTER 9

Defining Our Topics

*When truth is buried underground it grows. It chokes, it gathers such explo-
sive force that on the day it bursts out, it blows up everything with it.*

—EMILE ZOLA

Some issues are specific to particular time periods, but most continue
throughout the approximate 500-year development of the modern world.
Archaeological topics such as intercultural contact and ethnic diversity fueled
by immigration date from the earliest population movements until today. We
find the creation and dissolution of boundaries based on race, ethnicity, class,
and gender to be of vital interest, as is seeking the ways that people crossed
over or reinforced such boundaries. Tracing the interplay between changing cultural metaphors and the ways the people materially express such deep
beliefs also is relevant through the entire time period. In general the topic of
the transformation of everyday life is tied to changing economic and social
conditions, the evolution of technology, and environmental change.

Many types of sites are common to all time periods, including domestic
sites, farms, shipwrecks, military sites, gardens and other landscapes, and
cities. It is relatively rare that historical archaeologists seek out cemeteries
or burials for excavation, but their study provides important information on
demography, health and disease, and injuries or work stress.

Although many themes and topics continue to be archaeologically important through the historic period, there are some topics that receive more attention depending on the time period being investigated. For example, researchers
investigating exploration and early colonial settlement tend to be interested
in intercultural contact and influences between Native peoples, Europeans,
and Africans; colonists' relative self-sufficiency and reliance on their mother
country; and adaptation to both new ecological and social environments on

the frontier. Historical archaeologists are increasingly attentive to the experiences of Native and forcibly relocated African peoples and are working to understand the full complexity of the colonial period.

Increasingly, historical archaeologists are studying Native peoples' lives after colonization rather than only focusing on the initial period of contact and conflict with Europeans. In Australia, for example, those embracing the concept of a shared history are working to make the Aboriginal experience an integral part of the Australian national experience. One of the challenges to such shared history, of course, is that such different perspectives do not necessarily mesh into a single history. Some archaeologists and historians—both Native and non-Native—in the southwestern United States have adopted an approach that will probably become increasingly common. The articles collected in *Archaeologies of the Pueblo Revolt: Identity, Meaning, and Renewal in the Pueblo World* do not present one coherent whole. As editor Robert Preucel (2002:18) remarks, "What emerges, then, is not a single, definitive archaeology of the Pueblo Revolt, but rather multiple archaeologies of Pueblo resistance to Spanish colonial rule."

Depending on the region, time period, and colonial power, archaeologists focus on different economic, social, cultural, and religious institutions. The English, Spanish, French, and Dutch established forts throughout the American colonies to defend their land claims. Spain established Christianizing missions throughout its colonies. The British establish penal colonies in North America, Australia, and India, as well as workhouses and poorhouses at home and in the colonies. The Portuguese, Dutch, French, and British built or appropriated coastal forts in West Africa to guard their African cargoes prior to the Middle Passage of the transatlantic slave trade. Archaeologists are also interested in the establishment and development of towns and cities, some of which were intended to anchor colonial claims. Cities became increasingly important in political, economic, social, and cultural life in both colonies and mother countries.

Archaeologists studying colonies are concerned with the ways that people lived after the initial frontier period of colonization. Research on lifeways looks into how people fed and clothed themselves and the economic strategies by which they made a living. Studies of settlement patterns describe how people organize themselves across the landscape. At every scale, from house lot to city to region, such research can tell us about social and political relationships among economic classes and people of different ethnic groups or national origins.

It is relatively recently that archaeologists have begun to seriously study gender. The careful analysis of artifacts, informed by historical and anthropological understandings of women's and men's idealized roles, can shed light on how such roles changed through time.

Many archaeologists are interested in how enslaved Africans resisted slavery and maintained or adapted African cultural traditions. More interest is turning to the slave trade as a whole, both in Africa and elsewhere and in the triangle trade that moved people and goods between Africa, the Americas, and Europe. Slave-based plantations were fundamental to the economic and social landscape of the Caribbean, the American South, and South America from the earliest settlement through much of the 19th century. Of course, there were also slave-based plantations and farms in the northern North American colonies, but they are less thoroughly studied and remembered because emancipation of slaves in northern states predated the Civil War, which has inspired so much American regional and national mythology as well as school curricula. Increasingly, our interest is turning to the lives of free people in the African diaspora.

In the 18th and 19th centuries new opportunities, particularly in the colonies and new nation, provided fertile ground for the establishment of utopian experiments. Both secular and sacred utopian groups provided alternatives to the culture rooted in industrial capitalism that was building like a tidal wave. It is important to study the successes and failures of such settlements to understand the wide diversity during a time period we often think of as fairly uniform.

During this time as well, earlier small-scale manufacturing yielded to full-blown industrial development. The archaeological remains of industries are often abundant. They include sites of mining, logging, manufacturing, transportation, food processing, and power and communication systems. Industrial sites range from a small-scale pottery shop and kiln site to a coal-mining district, and include the full range of factories, machines, canals, and residences of workers and overseers.

Archaeologists at some 19th- and 20th-century workers sites have identified ways that "scientific management" techniques of the time were used to try to divide and control workers and to enforce discipline and obedience to authority. Part of such management entailed assigning jobs according to ethnicity, color, and national origin. Indeed we often find evidence for ethnicity in Western work camps through specific foods and other items. Many industrial places have neighborhoods known as Chinatown or Little Rome. Early

FIGURE 2. This historic photograph shows workers and a steam shovel in the foreground of Alabama Gates Camp. (*Courtesy of Thad van Bueren*)

20th-century construction workers on the Theodore Roosevelt Dam on the Salt River in Arizona arranged their work camps in this way. The work camps occupied by Apache laborers, for example, yielded evidence of workers living in traditional wickiups. Everyday objects were modified to be used in traditional Apache ways. For example, the workers punctured metal buckets and cans to make strainers for brewing corn beer.

Such organization by ethnicity or national origin was not consistently the case, however. Construction workers building the Los Angeles aqueduct lived at the Alabama Gates Camp from 1912 to 1913 (see figures 2 and 3). Although an analysis of the architectural remains and camp layout revealed that the segregation of space was clearly ordered according to principles that divided workers by job status, archaeologists found no clear indications of the ethnic differences they expected. This finding is similar to what archaeologist Donald Hardesty found at the early 20th-century remains of Reipetown in eastern Nevada. This mining town reveals no evidence of internal class distinctions. Neither does the material culture indicate consumer differences among documented households of ethnic Slavs, Greeks, Italians, Mexicans, and Japanese.

In the United States, commerce, industry, agriculture, and regionalism increased during the Civil War. In its aftermath, Reconstruction and the Jim Crow era had a pervasive effect on race relations and the lives of both

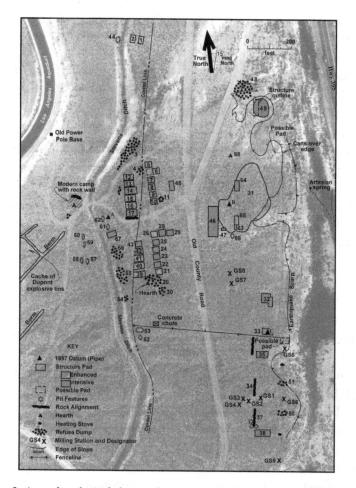

FIGURE 3. An archaeological plan overlain on an aerial photograph of Alabama Gates Camp shows the layout of the buildings carefully planned according to early 20th-century ideas about scientific management. (*Courtesy of Thad van Bueren*)

the native-born population and the burgeoning immigrant population. More archaeologists are turning their attention to the 20th century, including Depression-era sites and sites of industry and the tensions and violence between labor and capital.

Archaeologists also study people's lives today. Some explicitly use the field's methods as a way to help people cope with the ongoing effects of the very recent past, such as state violence in concentration camps. Some of the many horrifying places that forensic archaeologists have worked are the processing centers from which the military government in Argentina "disappeared" at least 9,000 people between 1976 and 1983 (hence my choice of quote for the start of this chapter).

Archaeologists also study the ways that we make, buy, and use modern material culture. While questions we ask about our current relationships with the things appear to be endless, archaeology often provides a fresh look at our modern lives. We argue that material culture and consumption play active rather than passive roles, affecting the social relations of ethnicity, gender, and race. Some archaeologists see themselves as performing a kind of object-centered psychoanalysis of our Western culture, which is certainly object-obsessed. Artists such as Mark Dion claim to do archaeology, and their portrayals often highlight very interesting (and, to archaeologists, sometimes painfully stereotypical) aspects of our work.

Interwoven with all of these topics is the meaning of the work; the connections between past, present, and future; the pursuit of *sankofa*. For example, the group of archaeologists who identify themselves as the Ludlow Collective investigate the site of the Ludlow Massacre, where striking coal miners and their families were killed by the Colorado National Guard in April 1914. They are interested not only in documenting the material evidence of the tent colony and its destruction, but also in reviving the memory of working-class struggle by commemorating this event, which sparked an important turning point in labor relations in the United States.

I've swept through our topics as a way to frame the rest of this book. Every topic contributes to at least one, and often more than one, of our general goals. In the next chapter I discuss some of the overarching topics connected with our goal of understanding modernization and globalization.

CHAPTER 10

Colonialism, Capitalism, and Slavery

It's an interesting question, "When is Now?" "Now" can be drawn from some point like this hour, this day, this month, this lifetime, or this generation. "Now" can also have occurred centuries ago; things like unfair treaties, the Trail of Tears, and the Black Hawk War, for instance, remain part of the "Now" from which many Native Americans view their place in time today. Human beings respond today to people and events that actually occurred hundreds or even thousands of years ago.

—ANTHONY F. C. WALLACE

The past is never dead. It's not even past.

—WILLIAM FAULKNER

Colonialism is a power relationship based on exploitation of the colonized by colonizers. It works through military power—there is good reason, after all, that so many colonial settlements were first established as forts—but also through the political system, ideology, and especially economic system. Colonialism is not unique to the modern world. Depending on the resources to be exploited and the cultures of both the colonizers and the colonized, it takes on different forms in different nations. However, as a manifestation of European capitalism in the world, it does share certain features and invite similar research questions. For example, how do the purposes of colonists affect their relationships with the colonized? How do conflicting cultures affect and change each other? How do relationships with the originating countries develop? How do colonizers use slavery to make colonies profitable? How do the processes of acculturation, assimilation, and creolization work? How do we identify and analyze such complexities in the archaeological record?

It is also important to understand that, in order to justify exploitation, colonial ideologies—like any set of ideas that justify violence—denigrate the cultural worlds of the colonized and the enslaved. Because of this, the documentary record is unlikely to provide an unbiased or complete view of the "other." Part of what archaeology can do is provide access to more of the past. It can give voice to those who were muted by the colonial system and counter the long-standing legacy of colonial ideology that categorized the colonized as uncivilized and unworthy.

In addition to economic, political, social, and ideological effects, colonialism leaves a biological and spiritual legacy. European diseases severely depopulated the Americas. Children of mixed parentage, whether or not of marriages, are the common biological legacy of colonialism. The ways that these individuals were treated varied widely and historical attitudes toward such "mixing" continue to haunt social relationships.

Numerous explorations and expeditions provided European states with information about the lands that would become their colonies. They also provide archaeologists with invaluable, albeit incomplete and biased, descriptions about Native peoples' lives at the time of European contact and about some of the Native reactions to their expeditions. For example, Hernando de Soto made his *entrada* in what is now the southeastern United States in 1539. Archaeologists and ethnohistorians have reconstructed the routes traveled. They have succeeded in identifying some of the archaeological remains of the powerful chiefdoms encountered, including those of the Coosa province in northwestern Georgia, and those of Anhaica, the Apalachee village in Florida where the Spaniards spent the winter of 1539–1540. A generation later, the Tristan de Luna Expedition in 1560 and the Juan Pardo Expedition in 1566 also explored the region, visiting some of the same places and providing some further descriptions of the towns and people.

There are examples of such documentation in every region the Europeans explored. Samuel de Champlain, for example, wrote copiously and drew detailed maps reporting on his travels in what is now the northeastern United States and southeastern Canada from 1604 to 1608. Jacques Marquette and Louis Joliet recorded their exploration of the Mississippi River Valley in 1673. French colonists described some of the rituals they observed in the highly stratified society centered at the Grand Village of the Natchez Indians on the Mississippi River, occupied before 1682 until 1730. From 1804 to 1806, the travels of Meriwether Lewis and William Clark provided an extraordinary snapshot of parts of the soon-to-be-American West.

One of the major mistakes that archaeologists have made is to think about Native societies in the protohistoric period between "prehistory" and history, as if they were ahistorical and static. This misconception came directly out of 19th-century anthropology that assumed cultural continuity and developed the "direct historical approach" to trace contact-period cultures back to their "prehistoric" authenticity. Such an approach assumes a clear continuity between present and past, forgetting that all cultures change over time. The way that the direct historical approach was conceptualized strengthened the widely accepted colonial assumption that Native cultures were doomed to disappear.

Archaeologists have begun to reconceptualize what it means to study Native Americans during the historic period. Patricia Rubertone, for example, has critically analyzed the way that the legacy of the direct historical approach has limited historical archaeological study of Native cultures. In her book *Grave Undertakings: An Archaeology of Roger Williams and the Narragansett Indians,* she demonstrates a different approach. She investigates how the Narragansett in the early Rhode Island colony found inventive methods to maintain cultural continuity in the face of constant Puritan pressures to become like English Christians.

Understanding that Native peoples' lives and struggles are worthy of study will change the questions we want to ask about colonization. How do cultures under threat of military, economic, social, and ideological domination resist, adapt, cope, change, and survive? Such questions lead us to anthropological concepts of acculturation and creolization.

The concept of acculturation refers to culture change that occurs in response to long-term cultural contact. Although it was not originally defined as asymmetrical change involving transmission solely from one culture to another, in practice, the term came to imply that Native or other dominated cultures accepted the customs and values of the dominant European cultures. Archaeologists devised measures of acculturation based on the adoption of material culture. In retrospect, some of our models and results were limited and, frankly, biased to discover or confirm what we thought we already knew about the seemingly inevitable (and even eager) acceptance of European culture. However, it eventually has become clear that cultural change through contact occurs in different ways and paces in different situations. Our conceptual language was starting to stand in the way of innovative investigation. In response, several archaeologists working with intercultural influences, particularly among African, Native, and European cultures, proposed that historical archaeologists should be thinking more about "creolization," a concept that received increasing attention from the social sciences in the 1990s.

There is no agreement among archaeologists on the precise definition of creolization, but at minimum it refers to a mixing or hybridization. Some archaeologists adapt models from linguists' findings about the ways that Creole languages develop and change. They look for an integrated mix of cultures that are coming together. Others adopt a model that analyzes change within the new and often volatile (and unpredictable) social, cultural, and natural environments encountered under colonialism. Those who use a biological model look for both physical and biological characteristics of a hybrid population. In chapter 20, I discuss some examples of creolized material culture.

Clearly, these models of creolization are not mutually exclusive, and they are most effectively used in combination and along with concepts of power relations and analytic techniques that are conscious of racism and ethnocentrism. As we study creolization we also must be aware of the fluidity of frontier and borderland societies. Individuals and groups manipulate their identities and the ways they present themselves to others; they compete and attempt to minimize both their individual and group disadvantages. Many of these complicated strategies leave clues in material culture.

The fluidity of the concept of creolization is important because it leaves possibilities open for new questions and new insights. It gains usefulness as a methodological tool as archaeologists connect it with other concepts. How might the process change as the relations of power change? Initially, there may be a shaky frontier where the threat of Native military action, poor supply routes, and unfamiliarity with local environments and resources all combine to require diplomacy and trade. Contrast this with the situation of a stable settlement where a "pacified" Native population has become all but invisible to settled colonists. How do cultural interactions change as a colonizing culture, for example, solidifies its military dominance and enforces racist ideologies?

Consider the long-term colonialist contact between the self-defined "civilized tribes" of southeastern Native Americans and European Americans during the early 19th century. The tribes both adopted and rejected Anglo-American objects and their uses. European dominant ideology embraced a set of ideas about the progress of civilization. The Cherokee, for example, responded by establishing a capital for their independent nation, as well as a constitution (in 1827), a republican government, their own writing system, printing press, a national newspaper, a Christian church, and a police force to protect property—in short, the explicit ingredients for what was understood to be "civilization."

What are the meanings of creolization in this setting? The Cherokee sought to introduce the possibility of heterogeneity to the European concept of civilization. The challenge was rational, reasoned, and logically sustainable. However, logic—and an alternative way of being "civilized"—was trumped by white settlers' desire for land and wealth. The U.S. Army evicted 16,000 Cherokee from their homes in Tennessee, Alabama, North Carolina, and Georgia, and in 1838–1839 forced them west on the Trail of Tears to what is now Oklahoma. This culmination of the Indian Removal Act of 1830 was meant to eliminate the threat to American cultural and "racial" supremacy, as well as to eliminate economic competition (gold had been discovered in the region). Certainly, in the long struggle of challenge and response, neither the dominant nor dominated group acted uniformly; their actions and desires were not monolithic. Rather, factions on each side were involved in intragroup power dynamics and ideological struggles.

The Cherokee resisted both the total destruction of their culture (ethnocide) and the creation of a new culture (ethnogenesis) that would be defined solely by missionaries, government agents, and other whites. Instead, the Cherokee's own ethnogenesis was of an altered Cherokee identity, although most of them had to ultimately continue their ethnogenesis on foreign soil far to the west, in what is now Oklahoma.

Conflicts in relations between Native, African, European, and Asian Americans began with first contacts and continued through the 18th and 19th centuries and beyond. Capitalism's increasingly pervasive promises were being made: in return for market participation, cultural assimilation, and conformity, individuals were to be allowed liberty and a place in the new republic. But racism, sexism, nationalism, and ethnocentrism were used to deny the promise to anyone defined as being on the disadvantaged side of the color and gender line.

Several archaeologists have suggested that capitalism be considered the proper primary focus of historical archaeology. Capitalism—the whole economic system and complex set of social relations—is important because it helps us to focus on the long-term development of the modern world. That is, this overarching question comes from contemporary life and the desire to understand how our current modern world came to be. Research on the complex and multifaceted phenomenon of capitalism seeks to understand the most pervasive changes of the past half millennium: how did people make sense of these economic, technical, and social transformations and their cultural effects?

I have spent some time summarizing colonialism as a topic. It should be clear that we really cannot separate colonialism from capitalism. Neither can be separated from slavery, which has a long global history stretching from the trans-Saharan slave trade to the Middle East and Mediterranean; to the transatlantic slave trade; to the illegal, underground global market for human beings today. An archaeology of slavery is not an archaeology of diasporic Africans, although it certainly includes that. Instead, it must also look at wealth created by slavery, from English country estates, to the homes of the United States' founding fathers, to middle-class inherited wealth.

For example, Susan Andrews and James Fenton describe the role of social ambition in fueling the slave trade. They look at the career of Enos Hardin in 19th-century Kentucky. An illiterate farmer, Hardin was nonetheless an astute businessman. He became wealthy and funded his climbing into a higher social status through his involvement in breeding and selling people. Slavery created and sustained supply and demand for far-reaching trade in commodities like tobacco, sugar, rum, rice, and cotton. Slavery and the slave trade, like colonialism (including the enslavement of indigenous people) and capitalism, infiltrated the whole of the developing modern world.

These phenomena are worldwide in scope, and historical archaeologists turn their attention around the globe to areas colonized or otherwise affected by Europeans. Neither capitalism, nor colonialism, nor slavery is monolithic; instead, regional differences in indigenous culture, historical contingencies, and ecological settings influence and are influenced by European-led economic conquest.

The quest for wealth all over the globe over the last half millennium has left us a complex legacy. The questions we ask about it are relevant to how we understand similar motivations today as we see multinational corporations expand to extract and process raw materials for a global market. The emerging modern world was different from our world today, but in it we can recognize, study, and begin to understand causes and consequences of past actions.

CHAPTER 11

What Is Our Evidence?

The humble tenacity of things
waiting for people, waiting for months, for years

—ADRIENNE RICH

As we've already seen, historical archaeology is a diversified discipline using a wide range of material culture, historical documents, and theoretical frameworks. It's helpful to think of material culture broadly as all sorts of things in addition to the range of broken and discarded artifacts recovered underground. Material culture includes all things that are somehow influenced by the culture that created them. Therefore, it not only includes objects excavated from below the ground, but also written and printed documents, artwork, gardens, landscapes, the built environment of structures and streets, and objects that survive in public and private collections. Thinking about it this way reveals the vast range of evidence we can draw upon to learn about the past (and present).

Material culture conveys powerful messages. We take many examples of such culture for granted and follow their cues without much conscious thought. As a simple example, when I walk into a room where the chairs are organized in a block facing a stage or podium, I have a pretty good idea of the behavior expected of me there (sit down, listen, speak if invited). Another arrangement gives cues for different behavior. Messages of personal affiliation can be conveyed by clothing, from the "rally caps" of fans at a baseball game (Go Nationals!) to the purposefully intimidating "colors" of gang membership. Other messages may connect behavior with group membership and prompt questions such as: do I belong at this dinner party where I don't know what to do with the third fork?

Much of the archaeological record is underground or underwater. We describe archaeological context of below-surface remains three-dimensionally by horizontal and vertical associations and by the surrounding soils (the physical matrix). This gives us a way to keep track of relationships in space and time. Time may be indicated by stratigraphic layers in the ground, but also by "layered" alterations to a building or landscape.

Archaeological evidence consists of artifacts, ecofacts, features, and other physical remains in archaeological context and also, of course, historical documents and other evidence of the past, such as oral history and tradition. Artifacts generally can be picked up. They include such things as pieces of ceramic tableware, toys, machinery, toothbrushes, and the like. Ecofacts represent evidence from the natural world in archaeological context, such as pollen, phytoliths, plant parts, animal bones, parasites, and sediments. Features generally are not easily moveable. Features include buildings and structures, privy pits (latrines) and wells, and other remains such as foundations and the remnants of stockade posts or bridge piers. They may also be artifact concentrations such as trash scatters and dumps, or landscape features such as fencelines, hedgerows, mill tailings, or canals. The soil matrix surrounding artifacts and features is a source of evidence that provides information about the development of the site, including the effects of fires and floods.

It is fair to ask why it is necessary to excavate, when answers to research questions can be found in documents. However, much is not documented and, in general, the less documentation, the more we stand to learn from archaeology. But also, the sources of evidence are not equivalent and they may sometimes appear to disagree. Those who were writing documents often did not record the everyday, the taken-for-granted. In archaeology, the everyday is particularly important because it forms so much of our daily life and culture. James Deetz makes the case for broadening the sources of history beyond records left by an elite and literate subset of society. He writes:

Archaeology certainly can provide insights into historical processes that written records simply do not provide. Historical archaeology deals with the unintended, the subconscious, the worldview, and mind-set of an individual. It provides access to the ways all people, not just a small group of literate people, organized their physical lives. If only the written records, rich and detailed as they are, are studied, then the conclusions will reflect only the story of a small minority of deviant, wealthy, white males, and little else. I do not think we want that for our national history; therefore, we need archaeologists to find what was left behind by everybody, for every conceivable reason. The unintentional record of people provides scholars with ways to determine the underlying reality of our history. (1991:6)

Interpreting material culture depends upon archaeological context. Without such context, the value of artifacts is limited to aesthetic opinion and market price. Every archaeology student is told repeatedly that without context, artifacts are meaningless because they have lost their information value. Similarly, the contexts themselves are broad. They encompass not only the archaeological context of provenience described in terms of excavation units, stratigraphic levels, and features, but also societal and cultural patterns. As the questions become more complex, we require broader contexts to frame and address them.

Scholars in several disciplines beyond archaeology, such as the history of technology, architecture, materials science, and art history, are interested in artifacts. Because objects are central to human expression, material culture studies has emerged as a distinct interdisciplinary field of study. Under this umbrella, many disciplines are making the leap from studying isolated objects to a more comprehensive look at meanings of objects in broad contexts.

Historical archaeologists struggle to find ways to effectively use both material culture and documents to create more realistically broad and inclusive histories. The specific uses to which documents may be put to aid interpretation range from the identification of objects and their uses to the explication of a culture's worldview. For example, documents may help identify artifact functions (is it a butter dish or gravy boat?), date specific forms or maker's marks (a plate with a registration mark from a potter in business from 1862 to 1889), and name objects according to contemporary typologies (for example, this size plate is called a "twiffler" or this type of ship is a "galleon"). Documents such as maps or travelers' accounts may also help to identify the location and identity of sites.

The documents studied range from official to private to literary. Their sheer variety and volume are enough to make one's head spin. Maps, architectural drawings, plans, period artwork, and photographs are invaluable. Useful government documents include official papers, policy documents, court records, and statistics such as census, taxes, and production figures. There are explorers' and travelers' accounts; mission and church records; and letters, diaries, and private papers. There are also business and company account books, personnel records, union records, and insurance files.

Literature, including travel literature both by outsiders and locals, as well as fiction, novels, short stories, plays, and poetry, is underused by archaeologists to understand the cultural contexts of the past. Ephemera such as newspapers, pamphlets, brochures, broadsheets, directories, catalogs, and other mass media with a limited circulation or life span are frequently used when collections are easily accessible and, preferably, indexed. Transcripts or tapes of oral history interviews are becoming increasingly important, particularly for studies of the recent past and contemporary meanings of history.

Archaeological and documentary evidence are not equivalent. They are created over very different spans of time and with very different intentions. What's more, they can appear to contradict each other so it can be tricky to use them together to create a whole greater than the sum of its parts. However, the interplay of evidence is productive and leads to questions worth asking. In the Chesapeake region of the Mid-Atlantic United States, archaeologists have been making a concerted effort over several decades to build a database of animal bones found in the archaeological record. By analyzing these faunal remains, archaeologists describe animal husbandry, butchery and food preparation, dietary practices, and the marketing and distribution of animals and animal products.

Bones, therefore, can reveal a great deal, but historical sources are also needed to get a complete picture. Probate inventories (lists of possessions made at the time of death) and tax lists show the animals kept by urban households. Store accounts show what was available for purchase. The laws governing the marketplace are found in municipal records. Plantation accounts can reveal how livestock were raised and brought to market, while household accounts can document specific purchases. Historical analysis provides recorded social and economic contexts about consumption, and the archaeological remains reveal what different households actually consumed. Very specific questions—such as, what part of what animal is this bone from?—demand very precise answers. They are the building blocks necessary for addressing big, overarching questions such as: What did it mean to live in a modern, urban-based, market economy? What was the quality of life in rural and urban colonial and early America?

I want to emphasize ethnography as another source of evidence for historical archaeology, largely because we don't often take advantage of its potential. Amy Young, Michael Tuma, and Cliff Jenkins investigate the lives of African Americans on the Saragossa Plantation just outside of Natchez, Mississippi, through archaeology, oral history, and study of the descendant community's traditions. The Saragossa Plantation operated from 1823 until the end of the U.S. Civil War. Like other cotton plantations, Saragossa was home to a shifting and growing enslaved population that needed to invent ways to create viable communities as individuals and members of families came and went as they were bought and sold.

The researchers are particularly interested in how people minimized the risks and dangers in their environment in order to live. Enslaved people used a variety of strategies for reducing risk. For example, they might attempt to prevent or manage loss and food shortages through taking suckling pigs for their own use, storing and thereby controlling food in root cellars beneath cabin floors, and sharing food and other goods by establishing reciprocal obligations and strong family and community ties.

At Saragossa, as at many other plantations, animal bones excavated from cabins indicate that meat came predominately from domestic animals, especially pig, but also cattle, and sheep or goats (archaeologists record sheep/goats because the bones of these species cannot be readily differentiated). However, evidence of wild species—including deer, squirrel, raccoon, rabbit, and various fish and other aquatic species such as turtles—indicates that enslaved workers hunted to supplement whatever food was provided to them.

In order to better understand the social roles of hunting in the rural African American community of Saragossa, Michael Tuma "apprenticed" himself to local African American hunters who were willing to teach him how to hunt. He quickly realized just how important hunting, fishing, and trapping were as vital male-bonding activities. As a group activity in this community, hunting requires cooperation. Successful hunters share the meat through a communal feast and then distribute remaining meat to others to freeze for future use. Such long-term traditional meaning of hunting and the social practices surrounding it have helped the archaeologists to understand some of the bonding and sharing that might have been going on in the past and to figure out how to research it in the archaeological record.

Young and her colleagues analyze a range of evidence, both past and present, to discover how hunting was not only about having enough to eat. Hunting at the plantation was also a strategy of risk management that enslaved men used to regain some limited measure of control over their lives, as well as to cope with meager rations provided by slave owners. Men also hunted to support male gender identity, and hunting served as a way to incorporate strangers, such as those recently purchased, into the enslaved community.

An archaeology of enslaved life requires that we understand the ambiguity and difficulties of our evidence. How, for example, might we recognize and interpret resistance to oppression, alternative lifeways, or unexpected behavior? In considering evidence and what it means, I turn in the next chapter to the challenges of identifying expressions of people whose voices are difficult to hear.

CHAPTER 12

Ideology, Ambiguity, and Muted Groups

It was the best of times, it was the worst of times, it was the age of wisdom, it was the age of foolishness, it was the epoch of belief, it was the epoch of incredulity, it was the season of Light, it was the season of Darkness, it was the spring of hope, it was the winter of despair.

—CHARLES DICKENS

Alternative values may be expressed in material culture, but they are not often easy to find. In 19th- and 20th-century North America, the dominant culture's Enlightenment values appear to be expressed in the consumer culture of the industrial revolution, making it very difficult to observe diversity through artifacts. For example, in their study of the Depression-era Aiken Plateau in South Carolina, Melanie Cabak and Mary Inkrot found that wealthier households may have spent more on services such as domestic help and gasoline, but that most households in the community spent similar amounts on consumer goods. They explain (1997:190): "Although very few households could afford to mechanize their farmsteads or modernize their homes, most people, regardless of tenure class, had access to inexpensive consumer goods, such as soda pop, that were being produced by the nation's expanding factories."

We need to resist the temptation to interpret such similar material goods to mean similar ways of thinking. From a simple reading of material things, mass-manufactured goods imply mass-manufactured culture. It is one of the challenges of historical archaeology to decode the complexities of consumption within consumer culture. Archaeologists must learn to interpret variable artifact assemblages and data that do not "fit" expectations as something meaningful rather than just "noise" in a predicted pattern. The following illustration of the ambiguity of artifacts and the expression of gender at two different sites should clarify the nature of the challenge.

Janet Brashler interprets late 19th- and early 20th-century logging camps in West Virginia. Historic photographs show that women and children were present at many larger logging sites. In contrast, smaller sites appear to have been occupied by men only. The presence of decorative, fragile glass and ceramics also shows the presence of women and heterosexually based families in larger logging camps but not at the smaller sites. A strong cultural metaphor connects women as "gentle" and "civilized" with the presence of fragile household objects.

Elizabeth Kryder-Reid analyzes gender relations at the St. Mary's site in Annapolis, Maryland. An all-male cloistered religious order—the Redemptorists—have owned this property since the middle of the 19th century. Kryder-Reid suggests that gender roles were implicitly assigned within the community, corresponding to a spiritual and authoritative hierarchy. Young men in training for the priesthood were expected to be of "manly courage" (explicitly expressed in Redemptorist writings), adopting masculine characteristics. Lay brothers, who would never attain the same spiritual authority, were given the domestic chores and supportive, traditionally feminine roles.

Cultural perceptions of household normalcy depend on their gender relations. It is worth asking, for instance, why Brashler's all-male logging communities owned few or no ceramics while an all-male religious community owned a collection of tablewares and teawares very much like contemporary middle-class households in the same city. Consider that, in contrast to the loggers, the male priests and brothers had differently engendered their own (nonsexual) relationships. The Redemptorists had no need to avoid feminizing artifacts while the loggers did in order to conform to cultural expectations about masculine and feminine behavior. I have a hunch that to adopt women's things at a single-sex and single-gender (male) site, would be to subvert "normal" hierarchy and relationships. It would serve to inappropriately (within the culture of the time) engender a single-sex community by implying a gendered hierarchy. The religious community instead supported a hierarchy imbued by the gender hierarchy embedded in the broader society. I imagine that the temporary nature of the camps also made it easier to forego the ideologically powerful gender hierarchy. Redemptorists expected to remain in their single-sex communities; loggers did not.

I want to think this through a little further in relation to some of the larger cultural processes that we understand about modern life. Consider that perhaps during the 19th and early 20th century nearly everyone within the European global market owned ceramic tableware and teaware because it was, in most cases, culturally appropriate to do so. One alternative, that of owning no appropriate equipment, would result in being defined as without "normal" gender relations, as with Brashler's male loggers, but not for Kryder-Reid's male religious group. Muted groups are those who are prevented from expressing their preferences and worldviews in the dominant cultural discourse. The mass-manufactured material culture thus draws them into the underlying expressions of the dominant culture.

The idea of a dominant ideology is useful here, but it requires some further refinement. This idea has been rightly criticized as unrealistic when dominance is assumed to pervade all parts of society and influence all individuals equally. Our own daily experience makes us quite skeptical of such a claim because we observe that individuals understand power relationships quite differently. Some believe all the claims made about them (pro and con) and others reject such claims. It is also worth remembering that ideologies are not restricted to dominant groups. It is useful to distinguish between a dominant ideology that is imposed through power (also called "vulgar ideology") and a hegemonic ideology that is widely internalized and regarded as kind of cultural "common sense" (also called "nonvulgar ideology").

Dominant or vulgar ideology refers to subjective knowledge and explanation that serves some social class, promoting, possibly through distortion, the dominant group's interests. Such ideology is potentially obvious and may be penetrated by individuals who can recognize, if not effectively resist, the ideological "arguments" used to maintain the status quo. An obvious example is the "scientific racism" of the 19th century, in which bad science propped up racist eugenics. Many of those being defined as inferior probably knew better but often were powerless to protect themselves. A less obvious example is the apparently widely held belief that material wealth legitimizes social power. Although the nonwealthy may question the message, they may not necessarily overturn it. The wealthy, however, may completely internalize the message, making it for them a matter of cultural common sense.

Hegemonic or nonvulgar ideologies as culturally embedded "common sense" constitute apparently objective knowledge thought to be beyond question. Such ideology is much more difficult to penetrate because it forms the basis for accepted truth. Muted groups may well see through dominant vulgar ideology and accept or reject it, but neither muted nor dominant groups are likely to perceive explicitly the structure of all hegemonic, often naturalized (and dogmatically defended) ideology. Examples of nonvulgar ideology are often revealed if we can manage to see ourselves through others' eyes.

Anthropology is a good source of other cultural "realities" that challenge our own. So is an anthropological history and archaeology that allows us to see alternatives. For instance, the concept of time as linear is a Western bit of cultural common sense that is not necessarily accepted by Native cultures, who may experience and describe time as cyclical.

In the model of muted groups, subordinate groups have little power with which to make any effective challenge to dominant groups, who generate and control the dominant modes of expression. An effective challenge is one that is heard, taken seriously, and responded to. Muted groups remain so not only through coercion, but also because their models of reality and worldview cannot be expressed adequately through the modes and ideologies accepted by dominant groups. Mutedness is a result of the relations of dominance that inhibit the expression of alternative models.

Muted groups who resist the dominant ideology must express themselves in ways that they perceive to be effective but not overly dangerous. If muted, then groups may express themselves in alternative media, for example, particular choices or uses of material culture, distinct rules of etiquette, or religion. Or they may refuse the dominant modes of expression by refusing to understand them.

The historian Mechal Sobel provides some examples that illustrate this sort of resistance by 18th-century women and enslaved Africans. She notes that "members of the [Virginia] elite often found that their wives and children did not share their preoccupation with redeeming time…. William Byrd II accused his first wife, Lucy, of not living up to 'proper' norms, of being negligent and disorganized, and of not 'improving' her time as he sought to improve his own" (Sobel 1987:65). In Maryland in 1736 Edward Kimber observed that if "a new negro…must be broke…. You would really be surpriz'd at their Perseverance; let an hundred men shew him how to hoe, or drive a Wheelbarrow, he'll still take the one by the Bottom, and the Other by the Wheel" (in Sobel 1987:47).

Muted groups have little choice but to express themselves through dominant groups' ideology and modes of expression or risk ostracism, condemnation, belittlement, or violence by embracing their own. Material culture provides a stage and a medium for expressing and learning cultural constructions. However, because muted groups operate within a society that gives them little means of expression, it is difficult to discover their muted voices. Historical archaeologists continue to learn to recognize these voices and to create appropriate concepts and methods with which to reveal them.

Consider the challenge of interpreting the material culture of nondominant groups whose power is limited and whose frequent poverty affects the household goods. Historically in the United States such groups include Native Americans marginalized on reservations, African Americans restricted by the black codes that kept them legally disadvantaged, Chinese immigrants concentrated in Chinatowns, Irish immigrants in inner-city "slums," and many others bounded by ethnicity, economics, or belief. Artifact expressions of culture designed to be misread by those in power are predictably difficult to even notice, let alone interpret. They are the expressions of muted groups conscious of the power of material culture in social interaction. Archaeologists finally have been able to see more clues of such expressions and only begun to make sense of these kinds of subtleties of the archaeological record. We have been able to do so because we have begun to see the people behind the artifacts as players in all scales of historical dramas. As we'll see in several examples throughout this book, historical archaeology contains particularly strong data with which to address strategies of coping with powerlessness and to discover the subtle expressions of mutedness.

CHAPTER 13

Ethical Considerations

Anyone who isn't confused here doesn't really understand what's going on.
—ANONYMOUS

Archaeological ethics can be complex and confusing. Responsibilities extend to the archaeological record, many different publics, and one's colleagues. As Randall McGuire points out, the development of cultural resource management over the last few decades has turned archaeology into a business, something that it really hadn't been before. Such growth raises ethical issues involved with "the relationship of research to legal compliance, the relationship of academic archaeology to business, the training of students, publication, and public outreach" (McGuire 2003:viii). In the academic realm, ethical issues surround teaching and treatment of students. Similar issues extend to one's coworkers. Archaeologists have slowly become aware of serious imbalances and stereotypes (based on race and sex especially) that adversely impact the whole field by affecting the kind of work individuals are trained and encouraged to do.

In this chapter I provide very brief characterizations of some categories of ethical issues. At the end of this chapter is a list of major professional organizations with ethics statements and URLs to find their current statements on-line.

Conservation of the Archaeological Record

Even though the archaeological record in a general sense is being continually created, archaeological remains are nonrenewable in the sense that such records of the past cannot be re-created. Many sites are destroyed or damaged by economic development—ranging from agriculture, to dam and road construction, to suburban subdivisions and urban renewal—or by looters who mine sites for artifacts they can sell or keep for their own collections. Casual collectors, recreational off-road enthusiasts, or divers can also damage sites, often unwittingly.

Some governments respond to the looting problem with creative and sometimes effective solutions, but the motivation for collecting ensures that the problem will continue. In the United States, the National Park Service and the Bureau of Land Management, for example, run sting operations to catch traffickers in illegally acquired artifacts. Vigorously prosecuting violations of the law is one tactic, but of course most archaeological remains are not protected by law. Public outreach and encouragement of public stewardship is another tactic for preservation. Through training programs for amateur archaeologists, several states accomplish a great deal of professional-quality work and dramatically expand public awareness of and concern for the looting problem. Another tactic is to remove sites from the marketplace to reduce the likelihood of looting. Based on the principle of the American sanctity of private property, the Archaeological Conservancy as a private foundation protects sites by purchasing them.

Site preservation was not always a widespread concern in the profession. However, rapidly increasing threats to sites caught the attention of both the profession and the public. Archaeologists have come to recognize their responsibilities to the record of human heritage and, importantly, to the peoples whose heritage is chronicled in archaeological sites. That responsibility extends to collections made from sites, as well as to the sites themselves.

Archaeology as cultural resource management (CRM) done under public law does not often result in the preservation of sites in place. Instead many sites are identified and judged insignificant according to legal standards and professional judgment. If judged insignificant, then sites are destroyed to make way for roads, pipelines, or other public projects. Alternatively, sites may be judged significant and be excavated in order to recover important data. Rarely are sites preserved in place if they are in the way of a development project. The stakes are high. Practicing archaeologists have an important ethical responsibility to be well informed and to do their work conscientiously. Their recommendations reverberate well into the future (see especially the ethics statements of the American Cultural Resources Association).

Because much archaeological fieldwork in the U.S. today is undertaken to comply with public laws, archaeologists are accountable for the results of their work, often paid for by public funds. If the results of the work are not taken care of properly, it is difficult to justify spending public money. Archaeological curation has become a crisis, due to widespread and long-standing lack of attention by archaeologists to their ethical responsibilities for the long-term care and management of archaeological collections. Collections include not only artifacts, but also noncultural materials such as soil samples, radiocarbon samples, and floral and faunal material; associated records such as field notes, maps, photos, and laboratory data; digital data; and research results such as site reports and publications. Everyone involved in creating collections is responsible for their proper curation. Without proper care, the essential archaeological information is likely to be lost because collections will disintegrate, disappear, or become so disorganized that they are unusable.

Diverse Publics

Archaeological places and the collections that come from their study are not simply resources full of data, but are places and objects of cultural heritage to living people. Using sites and artifacts for such purposes as education, community cohesion, entertainment, and economic development can lead to widespread benefits but also to conflict. For example, sites can be places of economic potential as heritage tourism destinations. Resulting interest in development can conflict with preservation or the desires of other interested publics, some of whom might not want visitors.

The use and abuse of science is a long and disturbing story. Scientific racism has left a bitter legacy, including the treatment of Native American human remains, which has been a major source of conflict between archaeologists and Native Americans. The ongoing tension between archaeology and the people whose past is studied concerns the ownership of the past and the worldwide issue of intellectual property rights. It is part of the ethical code of most professional archaeologists that the past belongs to everyone, but ethics and values often differ between tribes and professional archaeologists.

Historical archaeologists are not as directly affected by the Native American Graves Protection and Repatriation Act (NAGPRA) as their colleagues who study earlier Native American cultures. However, the ethics of dealing with descendant communities and the interested public apply to all archaeologists, regardless of the legal framework. The African Burial Ground project in New York City—the source of my *sankofa* theme—has been important for historical archaeologists because it brought to the forefront for discussion and debate our responsibilities to descendant communities. I'll touch on this project again in chapter 27.

Public Outreach

Professional archaeologists often criticize each other for their poor record in communicating with the general public. Because public outreach has not been part of professional academic responsibilities, public attitudes toward collecting antiquities and ignorance about the real cost of looting have continued to counter efforts at saving sites.

Anyone reading the literature on public archaeology will find that much of archaeologists' interest in public outreach stems from the need to protect and preserve archaeological resources. It should not be surprising, then, that the benefits of preserving sites often are couched in terms of benefit to archaeology through the creation of a public interested in and supportive of archaeology. In some circles, it has become fashionable for archaeologists to criticize the discipline and each other for their supposed limited self-interest in fighting for the protection of archaeological sites. But looting and destroying archaeological sites and other cultural remains is troublesome, and not only to archaeologists. We lose much more than a future for archaeologists with every destroyed site, every record of human achievement.

In the case of artifact trafficking, there is clearly a collision of ethical systems at work. Archaeologists might define it as a clash between business for profit and knowledge for the public good. Or perhaps it is a clash between aristocratic values of privileged personal ownership and democratic notions of common heritage. Where does the entitlement come from that allows one segment of the population to buy and thereby destroy another's history or sense of nation? Do we have (or want) common ground, or is world history just another commodity?

Preserving sites is essential if we are to preserve the public benefits of archaeology as national and local heritage. The malicious destruction of cultural identity came to worldwide attention (again) with the purposeful destruction of the Bamiyan Buddhas in Afganistan in 2001. The Taliban government was very explicit about its plans to destroy another religion's icons and cultural heritage when they announced their plans and then proceeded to destroy these monumental sculptures carved in the third and fifth centuries.

Archaeologists and curators have a responsibility to be aware of the ethical dilemmas that accompany armed conflict and its aftermath. Some of the unanticipated and unplanned-for consequences of the United States' wars in Afghanistan and Iraq has been the looting of museums, destruction and looting of archaeological sites, and the selling of artifacts on the international market. The Hague Convention of 1954 resulted from long-standing international efforts to protect cultural heritage in times of war. Its preamble states: "Damage to cultural property belonging to any people whatsoever means damage to the cultural heritage of all mankind, since each people makes its contribution to the culture of the world."

There is a direct connection between the destruction of sites by looters and the willingness of museums and private collectors to pay for the looted artifacts. Underlying tensions between the goals of museums and archaeology and their practitioners flare up around this issue, but the ethics of collecting need to be confronted by both serious and casual collectors as well.

There is more to public outreach than convincingly arguing for the preservation of sites and collections. The meaning of public archaeology is changing rapidly as archaeologists work more directly and more cooperatively with communities. Consider as well the challenges of making decisions about how to treat historic properties other than archaeological sites. Historic preservation is not just about preserving beautiful old buildings. It is also about the social responsibility of recognizing, preserving, and interpreting the full and inclusive breadth of our history. Archaeology's long-standing role in the broader world of historic preservation connects archaeologists to those decisions. Clearly, not every archaeological site or every standing structure can be preserved. The choices that are made daily by archaeologists and their colleagues in history and architecture require careful ethical consideration.

In their introduction to *Ethical Issues in Archaeology*, Larry Zimmerman, Karen Vitelli, and Julie Hollowell-Zimmer remind us that codes of ethics are neither static nor necessarily complete or final. Ethical practice needs to be based on ongoing critical reflection, discussion, and debate, and on an evolving process for reaching resolutions. I include URLs for various organizations' codes of conduct here rather than in the Further Readings section because I want you to consider them as part of this chapter. Ethics evolve to meet new challenges and therefore the organizations' websites will give you their most up-to-date versions. As you read them, you will probably notice that there are some conflicts between different organizations' statements. Some privilege the desires of associated groups of people; others privilege the archaeological record and associated information. Grappling with ethical issues can be frustrating. It is difficult but essential for anyone affected by these issues (that would be most of us) to work to apply ethical principles to the specific circumstances with which we are confronted.

Ethical Codes of Professional Organizations

United States
American Anthropological Association Code of Ethics
http://www.aaanet.org/committees/ethics/ethcode.htm

American Association of Museums Code of Ethics for Museums
http://www.aam-us.org/museumresources/ethics/coe.cfm

American Cultural Resources Association Code of Ethics
http://www.acra-crm.org/Ethics.html

Archaeological Institute of America Code of Ethics
http://www.archaeological.org/pdfs/AIA_Code_of_EthicsA5S.pdf

National Council on Public History Ethics Guidelines
http://www.ncph.org/ethics.html

Register of Professional Archaeologists' Code of Conduct
http://www.rpanet.org/

Society for American Archaeology Principles of Archaeological Ethics
http://www.saa.org/ABOUTSAA/COMMITTEES/ethics/principles.html

Society for Applied Anthropology Ethical and Professional Responsibilities
http://www.sfaa.net/sfaaethic.html

Society for Historical Archaeology Ethical Principles
http://www.sha.org/About/ethics.htm

International
Australian Association of Consulting Archaeologists Code of Ethics
http://www.aacai.com.au/codeofethics.html

Canadian Archaeological Association Principles of Ethical Conduct
http://www.canadianarchaeology.com/conduct.lasso

European Association of Archaeologists Code of Practice and Principles of Conduct
http://www.e-a-a.org/eaacodes.htm

International Council of Museums Code of Ethics for Museums
http://icom.museum/ethics.html

UNESCO International Code of Ethics for Dealers in Cultural Property
http://portal.unesco.org/culture/en/ev.php-URL_ID=13095&URL_DO=DO_TOPIC&URL_SECTION=201.html

World Archaeological Congress First Code of Ethics
http://www.worldarchaeologicalcongress.org/site/about_ethi.php

SECTION THREE

A Windshield Survey of Historical Archaeology

CHAPTER 14

Introduction to a Windshield Survey
of Historical Archaeology

The problem is not that we know more about less and less. The problem is that we know more and more about more and more.... The time will come when we know so much about so many things that no one person can hope to grasp all the essential facts...needed to make a single wise decision. Knowledge becomes collective in the weakest sense and science becomes like men and women in a crowd, looking for one another, each holding a single piece of a very expensive radio.

—MEL KONNER

It **is not** possible to provide a comprehensive summary of the contributions that archaeology has made to history, either globally or in the United States. Mel Konner's quote highlights a problem of the information age (beyond the obvious that technology has changed since he wrote *The Tangled Wing* in 1982!). It is particularly pertinent in considering the challenges of an inherently interdisciplinary approach like historical archaeology.

An archaeologist working on the Gulf Coast of the United States may find herself holding an important piece of the "radio"—perhaps some broken local earthenware, a few blue glass beads, a sherd of faience, and a chipped stone projectile point—and wonder where to find the other pieces. What kinds of recorded history might help? Should the search include oral history and if so, what source? The local communities? Which ones? Does she need to look for related clues elsewhere in the world? Where? What kinds of material science might identify the clay, the temper, the source of the stone, the source of the beads or the faience? In short, what pieces of the "radio" does one need to get a "transmission" from the past that is not hopelessly garbled? How can one tell when there is a coherent message?

As we've seen, one of the ways historical archaeologists organize their questions is to group them under large, interwoven topics like colonialism, capitalism, or consumerism. Or we may focus on sites occupied by people categorized by national origin, ethnicity, or race, or on particular kinds of sites, like urban or industrial or plantation. Or we might organize research geographically. The following chapters provide examples of a wide variety of questions for a global archaeology done one site at a time. This is a brief tour, a "windshield survey" that only hints at the breadth and depth of the work that has been done. I hope to raise questions and point to our connections with the present and future along the way.

CHAPTER 15

The Survival of the English Colony
at Jamestown

All the territorial possessions of all the political establishments in the earth—including America, of course—consist of pilferings from other people's wash. No tribe, howsoever insignificant, and no nation, howsoever mighty occupies a foot of land that was not stolen.

—MARK TWAIN

In 1607 just over 100 Europeans sailed up the James River and established a fort and settlement in the midst of Powhatan territory. It was not at all inevitable that Chief Powhatan or his people would let the colonists survive; certainly Jamestown could have gone the way of the failed colony of Roanoke just 22 years earlier. How, then, can the initial cautious but cooperative relationship that developed between the tribes and the colonists be explained? The study of power plays among colonial powers provides only part of the context of colonialism in the New World. The Native world was also full of complex characters and motivations. However, because of the limited view of European explorers and their records, much of this Native world does not appear in documentary history. We need a broader context that seeks to understand more about the Powhatan tribe's contemporary world. Archaeology helps to reveal that world.

Jeffrey Hantman studies Native responses to each other and to English colonists. He is fascinated by what he terms one of the more enigmatic events in the history of European colonization in the New World. This event is the generally tolerant reception of the Jamestown colonists by Chief Powhatan, the paramount chief of the Powhatan people of Tidewater Virginia. He explores the relationship between the Powhatans and their neighbors to explain part of the tribe's reaction to the English. His archaeological analysis raises important questions and possibilities for understanding the Native world during colonization by suggesting some ways that Native societies sought to gain from the presence of newcomers in their territories.

To understand what was happening in Tidewater Virginia in the early 17th century, we must broaden our perspective to include the whole region and a deeper past. The Monacan people occupied the piedmont territory west of the Powhatans' coastal territory of the tidewater. Although the English described the Monacans as principal enemies of the Powhatans in the early 17th century, the English and Monacans had little actual contact with each other. John Smith based his 1612 description of the Monacans and their neighbors on very few bits of evidence. Smith's writing provides a startling glimpse of the diversity of tribes and the complexity of political relationships in the region:

> Upon the head of the Powhatans are the Monacans, whose chiefe habitation is at Russawmeake, unto whome the Mouhemenchughes, the Massinnacacks, the Monahassanuggs, and other nations pay tributs. Upon the head of the river of Toppahannock is a people called Mannahoacks. To these are contributors the Tauxsnitanias, the Shackaconias, the Outponcas, the Tegoneaes, the Whonkentyaes, the Stegarakes, the Hassinnungas, and diverse others, all confederats with the Monacans though many different in language, and be very barbarous living for the most part of wild beests and fruits. (Hantman 1990:680)

Hantman analyzes Smith's language and word choice in linguistic and cultural context to remind us of the changing meaning of words and of biases inherent in such documentation. He reevaluates the common historical assumptions about the Monacans being inferior to Powhatans in social or political organization in light of contemporary English linguistic conventions, particularly concerning words like "barbarous." Seventeenth-century Europeans used the term "barbarous" to describe all non-Western, non-"civilized" people. However, Smith's use of the term has long been misinterpreted by anthropologists and historians to indicate that the Monacans were less civilized or less socially complex than the Powhatans, and therefore with less power and of less import during the colonial period. Archaeological evidence also effectively challenges the long-standing ethnohistorical (interdisciplinary study of Native people) characterization of the Monacans as "less complex" than the Powhatans.

To redress this inaccurate reading and to set the stage for his analysis of intertribal dynamics, Hantman reaches deep into the archaeological past. He looks at Monacan sites dating from around 800 to 1607 for evidence of settlement history, agriculture, and mortuary ritual and mound construction. Both the interior piedmont and the coastal tidewater appear to have had similar population densities, as settlements were concentrated nearly continuously along the James River through both physiographic regions. The distribution of settlements tells us that people started living in riverfront villages around 1000. The Monacans lived in a region with rich agricultural lands. Judging by the recovery of both maize and squash, they practiced farming, not relying upon (although certainly using) the "wild beests and fruit" as Smith reported.

At least 12 burial mounds attributed to the Monacans were built up from repeated use starting around 1070 and continuing until at least the 1400s and probably the 1600s. These mounds typically are situated on a floodplain near a large village, and they range from 400 to 625 square meters, standing up to five meters high. Hantman interprets the homogeneity of the mounds and other material culture to suggest a shared ideology and cultural continuity among the Monacans east of the Blue Ridge and related groups west of the Blue Ridge, with whom the Monacans traded. Hantman suggests that the Monacan people supported a hierarchical political organization with divisions between chiefly and nonchiefly lineages. In short, their social and political organization was every bit as complex (and unfamiliar to the English) as that of the Powhatans.

In re-examining the characteristics of the Monacans, Hantman essentially reintroduces them to the historical scene where we can begin to understand them as important players in the colonial drama. It is likely that the Monacans were a potent political force who worried Chief Powhatan. Their hosts told the Jamestown colonists that the Monacans were enemies who invaded the Powhatan lands. Further understanding of the competitive relationship between these chiefdoms requires that we consider a key piece of material evidence: copper. Copper was a powerful symbolic material in the Powhatan world. Before the English colonists came, one source of copper was the Blue Ridge mountains (known as Quirank), which was firmly within Monacan territory and control. The Monacans may also have played a key role in the exchange of more distant copper from the Great Lakes.

When the English came with their copper trade goods, Chief Powhatan himself monopolized that trade and gave the colonists corn in return, rejecting their offers of military alliance against his enemies. Chief Powhatan used his new source of copper to attempt to extend his control over less powerful local chiefs by carefully distributing the symbolically potent copper. Doing so increased these chiefs' own prestige and further indebted them to him. Chief Powhatan thereby dealt with the English through his own cultural strategies of alliance, using the foreigners strategically within the Native regional power struggle. With the English source of copper, Chief Powhatan no longer needed to trade with the militarily threatening Monacans. Therefore it was to his advantage to allow the English and their trade goods to stay.

Chief Powhatan's strategy worked temporarily, but individual English traders soon circumvented his control and flooded the region with copper. The prestige value of the metal decreased and its symbolic meaning disintegrated. At the same time, English colonists claimed more and more land for tobacco cultivation. In addition, a severe drought between 1607 and 1612 strained the resources of both Native and English settlers. Peaceful relations broke down. In one of many acts of resistance, the Virginia tribes coordinated a number of simultaneous attacks on March 22, 1622, an event documented archaeologically in the utter destruction of Wolstenholme Towne, commemorated and interpreted by Colonial Williamsburg. As the result of three Anglo-Powhatan wars and the deadly effects of smallpox and measles, the Powhatan confederacy had disintegrated by the mid-1640s, leaving scattered tribes in increasingly difficult circumstances.

Of course, the story of the Powhatans, the Monacans, and Jamestown doesn't stop there. Hantman has continued a different sort of work related to the Monacans, this time in collaboration with the present-day Monacan tribe. The archaeological research highlighting the importance of the tribe in the colonial encounters at Jamestown took on a significance that Hantman did not anticipate. Local media and the Monacan community, centered near Lynchburg, Virginia, picked up the message that archaeology could change present-day perceptions. Hantman's archaeological analysis, of which the Monacan community was unaware until after he completed it, helped shift the general public's perception of the tribe from a marginal player on the colonial scene to a central role. Interestingly enough, the Monacans' important roles in the past enhanced their standing in the present.

The Monacan community and Hantman have collaborated on grant writing and the design of a small traveling exhibit and video shown in both local public schools and the community heritage center. They also succeeded in listing the community's early 20th-century, missionary-run, log cabin schoolhouse on the Virginia and National Registers of Historic Places. These efforts make links between the past and present and bolster broader public recognition of Monacan identity.

FIGURE 4. African American archaeologists in the field laboratory at Jamestown Island, c. 1934. As a government-sponsored project in the 1930s, archaeology of Jamestown employed many people during the Depression. These African American laboratory technicians are some of the less familiar faces in the history of archaeology. (*Courtesy NPS Historic Photograph Collection*)

Returning to Jamestown Island, archaeological exploration of the fort and the town has been intermittent for over the past century, and recent work also has challenged some earlier ideas. On Jamestown Island, in 1893, the Association for the Preservation of Virginia Antiquities (APVA) acquired more than 20 acres surrounding the old church tower. In 1934 the National Park Service (NPS) acquired the rest of the island to establish Colonial National Historical Park and undertook extensive excavations (see figure 4). In the 1950s, archaeologists concluded that the fort had eroded away into the James River. However, William Kelso has directed APVA's Jamestown Rediscovery archaeological project since 1994. He and his associates have discovered remains of the triangular 1607 James Fort, including the palisade wall lines, the east cannon projection, several cellars, a building, and several graves. Only a portion of the fort has been eroded away by the James River, although it was accepted for years that the entire fort had been lost. Analyses of hundreds of thousands of artifacts dating to the first half of the 17th century reveal details and patterns of the early colony, including the discovery that the Virginia Company supplied the colony with up-to-date medical supplies and, tellingly, copper stock with which to fashion jewelry to trade with the Powhatans. You can get a good visual sense of Jamestown and its surroundings in 1607 from the 2005 film *The New World.* The filmmakers included archaeologists along with their other expert consultants and created, as accurately as currently possible, a picture of conditions at the fort and the material culture of both the English and the tribes.

The 400th anniversary of the founding of the Jamestown colony has inspired some very productive archaeology, as well as NPS and APVA plans to revisit and update public interpretation on Jamestown Island. In 2005 I happened to attend a presentation by an APVA spokeswoman about the organization's efforts to expand the stories that organization tells about the early colony. One important part of their effort is the inclusion of local Virginia tribes in the anniversary commemoration. I found it to be a fascinating presentation that highlighted issues of how we choose to include and exclude certain parts of the past and how we might overcome our blind spots. During the question and answer period I was very surprised by the remarks of one white man in the audience. He said, in effect, "If you're going to include the Indians, then there will be nothing there for me." In response to such a statement I ask myself if one story must necessarily overshadow another. How might on-site interpretation tell the "whole story"? Is it possible to tell the whole story?

CHAPTER 16

Mission San Luis de Talimali

Brother, you say there is but one way to worship and serve the Great Spirit.
If there is but one religion, why do you white people differ so much about it?
Why not all agreed, as you can all read the Book?
                    —SAGOYEWATHA (CHIEF RED JACKET)

Historical archaeologists have been investigating Spanish colonial sites
in the Southeast, Southwest, and West Coast of North America since the
1930s and have recently turned to such sites in Central and South America.
Mission sites in particular have captured both popular and scholarly attention.

The Spanish claimed the area from the Florida keys west to Mexico and
north to Newfoundland, but didn't settle much of that vast area that they
called *La Florida*. In La Florida, as in Jamestown, the earliest days of colonization were about accommodation and conflict between different ways of
life. However, both the goals and practices of the European colonizers and of
the Native Americans being colonized were different from Jamestown. In La
Florida a kind of cultural accommodation reigned for nearly 150 years, rather
than the brief period of accommodation in Virginia. Archaeologists trace the
terms of this accommodation in our studies of towns, missions, and burials.
While La Florida is not the Florida of today, the sites discussed here are in the
current state of Florida.

Well before the Spanish came to the North American continent, the
Apalachee in northern Florida were organized in a complex chiefdom with
social stratification. They were invaded by Hernando de Soto's army, who
set up winter camp from 1539 to 1540 in the Apalachee village of Anhaica, now recorded as the Governor Martin site in downtown Tallahassee. A
Portuguese officer who survived de Soto's 1539–1542 expedition through
the present-day southeastern United States wrote about the expedition. The

Gentleman from Elvas published his description in Portugal in 1557. Of the Apalachee, he wrote:

> On Wednesday, the third of March 1540, the governor [de Soto] left Anhaica Apalachee in search of Yupaha [a province said to have much gold]. He ordered all his men to provide themselves with maize for a journey of sixty leagues through uninhabited land. Those of horse carried their maize on their horses and those on foot on their backs; for most of the Indians whom they had to serve them, being naked and in chains, had died of the hard life they suffered during the winter. (1993:174)

A generation later, in 1565, the Spanish founded St. Augustine, the first permanent European settlement in the United States (San Juan in the U.S. territory of Puerto Rico was founded in 1521). St. Augustine was strategically located to protect the Spanish ships traveling through the Straits of Florida. It was also the hub of the southeastern mission network, which has a complex history during the 16th and 17th centuries. More than 100 missions were established from the 1560s until 1700.

San Luis was among the largest and most important mission sites in Spanish Florida and was established by the Franciscans in 1633. The first site of the mission, San Luis de Xinyaca, was probably near the site of Anhaica. At the instigation of the Spanish military, San Luis was relocated to its present site near Tallahassee in 1656 and, until abandoned in 1704, the San Luis mission was the western anchor of Florida's missions and served as the capital of western Florida. It was home to both a Spanish deputy governor and one of the Apalachee's most powerful chiefs. After 1670, ranching supported a community with a blockhouse and garrison, Spanish village, central plaza, mission church with burials, convento (monastery), the Apalachee chief's house, and the council house. San Luis was the only sizeable European population center beyond St. Augustine. The town planning indicates a high degree of incorporation and balance of both Spanish and Native elements: the Apalachee council house and Franciscan church were located directly across from each other facing the central plaza.

Bonnie McEwan surmises that both the Spanish and the Apalachee were maintaining parallel social and political institutions and also aspects of their traditional material life, but that there were also cultural exchanges. Native rulers met regularly at the council house, which served as the center

FIGURE 5. An archaeologist cleans off a cross-section after excavating one of the eight huge support posts of the original council house at Mission San Luis. Reconstruction was based on this and related evidence. (*Courtesy Mission San Luis, Florida Division of Historical Resources*)

of political, social, and ritual life. Investigations at the council house found remains of Native ceramics, projectile points, debitage from stone tool making, and a small amount of European material. At over 120 feet in diameter, supported by eight massive posts, the council house is the largest historic-period Native structure identified in the southeastern United States. The church was equal in importance to the council house. A cemetery with more than 900 burials of Christian Apalachee is under the floor of the structure. The chief's house yielded primarily Native material and included large numbers of quartz crystal beads and pendants. Southeastern Indians believed that quartz crystal held spiritual properties. The presence of these items reinforces the dual political and spiritual roles of Native leaders. At all the Hispanic households, Native pottery and food, especially maize, suggests the integration of Native women into the colonists' lives as servants, wives, and concubines.

I started this chapter with a quote by a Native American chastising Europeans about diversity of religion because religious differences, tolerance, intolerance, and missionizing are all important elements to understanding colonization and its legacy. Elizabeth Graham has studied mission archaeol-

FIGURE 6. The council house at Mission San Luis was reconstructed based on archaeological evidence. The council house was the center of Apalachee social, political, and ritual life. (*Courtesy Mission San Luis, Florida Division of Historical Resources*)

ogy in relationship to the Christianizing of the Americas. She observes that missions are usually depicted as the agents of imperialism, but cautions that some of their broader cultural impact is underappreciated. She is interested in "cultural imagination," that is, modes of perceptions and metaphors that lead to cultural understanding and ways of being.

Christian missions restructured the Native conceptual universe and did indeed serve imperialism by helping to underpin the new colonial order. However, Graham cautions against a simplistic historical interpretation that interprets the past in terms of either acceptance or rejection of Christianity. Instead, both the Native response and Christianity itself are more complex. Graham also insists that mission research should take into account the cultural imagination of Europeans, particularly the historical contradictions of European Christianity, which was neither uniform nor static but was characterized by variability and adaptation. Emphasizing that Europeans have no more claim to Christianity than any other people, Graham sees the adaptive history of the religion in the New World similar to that in the Old World, because in both places it was marked by changing practices and the incorporation of traditional rituals.

Christianity also exposed the deep contradictions of colonialism. Because Native people perceived and understood differences between Christian principles and certain ways they were being treated, they could protest—sometimes even effectively—systemic injustice. It is important to distinguish between various forms of protest. Overt political protest and revolt shows up in documents. However, archaeology is needed to find protest where it is manifested more subtly in everyday religious expression, aesthetics, build-ings, and other forms of material culture. Such pervasive everyday forms of protest may be more effective than rebellion, partially because they are more widespread and persistent. Describing the interplay of old and new ideas and the effects of European ideas and practices upon Native cultures and societ-ies, Graham (1998:29) writes, "Resistance and protest occur alongside active reexamination of former values, together with the development of new con-cepts about the world that indeed receive European input, but are the product of indigenous minds."

Partly inspired by Graham's work, Bonnie McEwan examines religious conversion in La Florida. Because of long-term archaeological work on mis-sions in the region, she is able to synthesize results from excavations at seven missions. McEwan finds evidence for Native religious transformations and adaptations in both the documentary record and the characteristics of burials in the mission cemeteries.

Unlike in the rest of Spanish America, religious conversion in La Florida was largely voluntary. The people had lost faith in their native leaders, partly due to the ineffectiveness of Native religion against European diseases like smallpox. The Native leaders apparently were willing to cede religious author-ity to the Spanish friars while maintaining political authority. Results of the Spanish strategy in La Florida are seen in the town and mission of San Luis de Talimali, as described above, where Spain allowed two organizations to exist side by side: the Spanish Republic and the Native Republic, each with their own internal hierarchies.

Of course, the Spanish expected more than simple conversion to Christi-anity. They also expected allegiance and tribute in labor and goods. However, the friars generally did not interfere with Native practices unless they directly conflicted with Christian mores. McEwan contrasts burial practices among Christianized Natives at San Luis and other Florida mission sites, precontact Natives, and Spanish Catholics to study variation and shed some light on the effects on Spain's spiritual conquest.

Christianized Natives chose burial in consecrated ground, often beneath church floors. Individuals were laid out on their backs with hands folded across the body. Mourners marked the social status of the deceased in various ways, including by proximity to the altar and by the type and quantity of grave goods. Such practice conforms and contrasts to both Spanish Christian and precontact Native practice. Precontact elites would have been buried in mounds, while commoners were buried in or near houses. Instead of the body being extended, these burials would have been flexed or bundled. Spanish Catholicism, in contrast, would have forbidden grave goods except for priests, who were buried with a rosary.

McEwan surmises that one of the most compelling bits of evidence for successful missions in La Florida is their lasting impact. The Native Christianized population was forced to abandon the province in 1704 with the destruction of the mission through raids by the English and their Creek allies. The Apalachee population fled to another Catholic colony, taking up residence in French Old Mobile. The Talimali Band of Apalachee Indians now live in Louisiana and are still practicing Catholics.

San Luis de Talimali is designated as a National Historic Landmark and in 2006 Mission San Luis received a Preserve America Presidential Award in recognition of its importance for heritage tourism and education. The State of Florida purchased the site in 1983 and started the major research program that has made it a very thoroughly studied Spanish mission. Reconstructions, based on detailed evidence and the work of an interdisciplinary team, are the core of the public interpretation at the site. McEwan comments that the lessons learned through planning and carrying out the reconstructions are that these settlements were anything but primitive outposts. The size and sophistication of the public buildings are now literally envisioned and recreated. As they are no longer simply abstract historical concepts, the reconstructions give visitors a way to imagine the reality and impact of the Florida missions and the lives of the Native and European people who lived in them.

CHAPTER 17

Enclosure of the English Countryside

They hang the man and flog the woman
That steal the goose from off the common,
But let the greater villain loose
That steals the common from the goose.
                                    —ENGLISH FOLK POEM, CA. 1764

Late medieval to early modern England (from approximately 1400 to 1750) witnessed many social, economic, and cultural changes, including enclosure of the landscape and widespread changes in perceptions about land and goods. These changes are associated with the rise of rural capitalism, before the large-scale industrial capitalism of the 18th century.

The change from feudalism to capitalism is quite important for understanding the modern world. It is also well studied by some of our most influential social theorists, including Karl Marx, Emile Durkheim, and Max Weber. Matthew Johnson looks at that change through the lens of material culture as he traces enclosure of the landscape, transformations in both "polite" (or high-style) and vernacular architecture, and major changes in household goods. Paul Shackel studies the changing rules of etiquette during this period and somewhat later. He connects the new rules of dining etiquette in particular with the postmedieval "ceramic revolution," which produced and distributed new vessel forms and styles. The ceramic revolution peaked with the 18th-century marketing innovations of Josiah Wedgwood and the consumer revolution of the modern era.

The medieval agricultural landscape was comprised of strip fields and commons beyond and between cultivated fields. By custom, common lands were available for grazing, gathering firewood, and other uses. Enclosure was both a physical and legal process. It was the replacement of open fields and commons with a private, hedged, and ditched landscape. Legally, it was the replacement of land held with common rights by that of private rights only. Those being displaced expressed their opposition in various ways, from riots to folk culture (such as the bitter commentary of the poem used to open this chapter). The term "Leveller," which was applied to those throwing down fences and filling in ditches, was later applied to radicals in the English Revolution.

Different processes of enclosure in different landscapes took place over several centuries. For example, general enclosure peaked from 1450 to 1550 but occurred until 1700. When grain prices were down and the prices for wool and cloth exports were high, landlords depopulated the land by turning out tenants. They then enclosed open farming fields to turn them into grazing land for sheep.

At a much quicker pace during the early 17th century before the English Revolution, landlords drained the Fens around the borders of Norfolk, Cambridgeshire, and Lincolnshire to replace the economy based on the marshland with arable and pastoral farming. Local people bitterly opposed this action, which destroyed local rights and quickly dismantled the whole traditional way of life.

Piecemeal enclosure occurred especially in wood-pasture areas where peasants could exchange neighboring holdings to collect their land together. This type of enclosure is very difficult to study, as it was informal and didn't leave clear evidence on the landscape or in documentary records. Because it often preserved some common rights, it probably was less violently opposed than other forms of enclosure.

Parliamentary enclosure occurred after 1750 when land proprietors applied to Parliament for an Act for survey and enclosure. This legal action was encouraged by the rise in demand for agricultural produce that accompanied industrial development and the Napoleonic Wars. That is, the profitability of selling food to support both industrial workers and armies demanded high agricultural productivity. This form of enclosure occurred especially in areas where the local population had been strong enough to withstand earlier enclosures.

Enclosure created a cultural redefinition of the land. The changing agricultural practices concerned more than a polarization of classes. Enclosure challenged ideas about custom, that is, practices that had been in place since time out of mind. Ideas about community and tradition were contrasted with legalistic, externally imposed boundaries.

The traditional world knew class differences and struggles between landlords and tenants, but the large numbers of landless laborers created by enclosure was new. The 17th century was a politically volatile time in England with the Civil War, the short-lived Republic, and the restoration of the monarchy in 1660. In general, however, English social structure started at the top with the monarch. The social hierarchy was infused with the concept of patriarchy, as men were in charge of every social organization from the sovereign state to individual households. Beneath the monarchy in descending order were the aristocracy of titled landholders; the landholding gentry, who became the governing class in the preindustrial period, when they owned half of the land though they were only 2 percent of the population; yeomen, who were a socially middling class of tenant farmers with some security and wealth; husbandmen, who were less secure working farmers; and then servants and laborers, whose situations varied but who often had rights to common land. At the bottom of the social scale were "masterless men" who were outside the recognized patriarchal structure. These people included tramps, vagrants, and tinkers. The urban middling classes also had an ambiguous place in the system.

In 1524, an estimate put the laboring population at 20 to 30 percent of the whole. By 1688, that proportion had risen to 60 to 70 percent. Fear grew about these laboring poor and the rise of vagrancy, migrant labor, and begging. Institutional responses included the establishment of workhouses and convict colonies. What is now the state of Georgia in the United States was chartered by King George II in 1732 and operated as a colony for the resettlement of English debtors and the "worthy poor." It also functioned as a buffer between the English colonies and Spanish Florida. However, with the success of the American Revolution, Georgia was no longer available and England soon established Australia as a convict colony. The colonies became attractive to new settlers willing to leave their homelands for the promise of economic opportunity as well as religious freedom.

The long-term result of enclosure was an imposition of a more "modern" kind of economic rationality tied up with larger markets and profitability. Other kinds of closure were occurring as well, as can be expected in such a major cultural shift. From 1400 to 1800 there was a transformation in architectural styles, domestic comfort, and material affluence. In medieval houses, the distinction between public and private was less than today, and much of everyday living was done out of doors. One part of the transformation involved the acquisition of moveable furniture. For example, where benches had been built in as part of the architecture, moveable chairs replaced them. Pieces of furniture and other household items began to be produced and consumed as commodities.

Even as the middling classes were becoming more prosperous, it was not a foregone conclusion that more wealth would be spent on domestic interior comfort. Understanding this transition requires that we look at it in the context of secularization, patterns of social competition and display, and changing rules of etiquette. A new stress on fashion tied to middling classes fueled the rise of individualism, the separation of public and private, and the demand for consumer products. As less was produced within the household, each family had to get more of its necessary goods from outside. Merchants established permanent shops in market towns and villages.

Paul Shackel (1993:2) summarizes the changing etiquette, "Although today many people in Western society would feel uncomfortable rejecting time discipline, eating foods with only a knife, wiping their mouth on a table cloth, and not brushing their teeth, all of these behaviors dominated Western preindustrial society." Commodification placed goods in a secular rather than spiritual domain, thereby freeing individuals to acquire and accumulate.

Personally, I find it difficult to fully comprehend the preindustrial, non-secular thinking of premodern times. The worldview is thoroughly foreign, but the history of the fork illustrates the escape of an artifact to the secular domain of the commodity and makes the magnitude of the shift a little more real. The earliest documented European use of the fork was in Venice, after a Venetian man married a Greek princess in the 11th century and brought her home. She brought her forks with her, thus incurring the wrath of the church, which condemned their use as excessive and vain. When the Englishman Thomas Coryate returned from his Grand Tour of Europe in 1601, he brought home the fork and the new etiquette from Italy, where it had clearly caught on. Coryate reported that he was "rebuked from the pulpit for his impiety" (Shackel 1993:146). In 1611, Coryate described the appeal of the curious practice: "The Italian cannot by any means indure to have his dish touched with fingers, seeing all mens fingers are not alike cleane. Hereupon I myself thought good to imitate the Italian fashion by this forked cutting of meate, not only while I was in Italy but also in Germany and often times in England since I came home" (Shackel 1993:147). The use of forks as well as standard, individual place settings at the dining table was an invention of the modern world.

The development of such manners was concerned with more than hygiene. "Proper" behavior defined through the rules of etiquette established and reinforced relationships within and between groups. The struggle for social position is often played out in the realm of acceptable behavior and the correct equipment for displaying one's social position. In chapter 6, I referred to the invisible-ink strategy when I described changing burial practices observed in the 19th-century Weir family cemetery in Virginia. Changing rules of etiquette with requisite forks and plates provide another example of the general observation that goods and their meanings change when social hierarchy is threatened. To bring this argument back to the realm of landscape, consider what Tom Williamson writes about the great English country houses of the mid-18th century. Their parklike settings were a new style and often redesigned the hedged and bounded agricultural fields resulting from earlier enclosures. It is not surprising then that many deserted settlements (created when tenants were evicted) lie within the bounds of such parks. Williamson summarizes:

> The expansion of the economy associated with the consumer revolution of the mid-18th century brought growing uncertainties over the very definition of gentility, as the middle classes grew in numbers and wealth and themselves acquired gardens of sophistication. In an uncertain world, [Capability] Brown's landscape style, which consciously downgraded the importance of the garden, but affirmed that of the park, firmly asserted the traditional status of landowners. Only they possessed the raw materials necessary for a park's creation—land in abundance. (1998)

Enclosure of the countryside and contemporary changes in other areas of life resulted in new ways of thinking and acting, but the changes were not all-encompassing. Folk traditions and alternative cultural models also persisted. As they colonized the globe, British emigrants took along both old and new ideas about common and legal rights, ownership, social position, architecture, agriculture, foodways, etiquette, and the meanings of the goods they owned.

CHAPTER 18

Capitalism, the Georgian Order, and a Woman

One faces the future with one's past.

—PEARL S. BUCK

The 18th century witnessed a great many changes in Western culture and society: the political upheavals of the American and French revolutions; the rise of capitalism; the burgeoning of the slave trade; the technological changes of the industrial revolution; and the cultural developments in worldview, ideology, and social relationships.

In his widely influential *In Small Things Forgotten: The Archaeology of Early American Life,* James Deetz found material culture evidence in New England for what he described as the developing Georgian worldview. Deetz characterized the shift in worldview as a deep culture change from valuing community to valuing the individual. He saw it as a change from a medieval way of thinking to our modern one. Historical archaeologists enthusiastically took on Deetz's ideas and searched for material culture evidence to support them. Archaeologists have examined all categories of material culture—from architecture, landscape, and garden design to the equipment for serving meals to the layout of colonial newspapers. Some observable characteristics of such change are increasing segmentation, separation, and standardization, such as that seen in Anglo-American houses: hence the name "Georgian," from that symmetrical style of architecture that came into fashion during the reign of the three Hanoverian kings named George who ruled England from 1714 to 1820. Such changes were not limited to New England, to America, or even to British colonies. They were pervasive in Western culture, also showing up, for example, in Dutch colonies in South Africa.

Deetz suggested that the shift in worldview was tied to the 18th-century Age of Reason. As we've seen in the previous chapter regarding the enclosure of the English countryside, the shift from medieval to modern took place over a long period of time. Deetz thought of the shift from the theoretical perspective of a structuralist. That is, he adopted some assumptions about universal structures of the mind operating in binary pairs of opposites.

Many historical archaeologists embraced the structuralism that Deetz introduced to the field's literature and logic. The language of structuralist oppositions such as Nature to Culture, Communal to Individual, and Public to Private became widely used to form research questions and interpret results. It took a while longer for structuralist (or other) historical archaeologists to recognize and seriously consider the importance of the Female to Male opposition. The gender dichotomy was central to the structuralism that became mainstream in historical archaeology, but its implications were all but ignored. Gender ideology is also of central concern in poststructuralist thinking and, of course, in feminist scholarship.

Mark Leone reacted to the essentially ahistorical explanations of structuralism and sought to add historical cause and effect to the structuralist framework. Instead, he suggests an emerging culture of capitalism as responsible for the range of changes that Deetz and others observed in New England. Leone established the Archaeology in Annapolis project in Maryland in the early 1980s to investigate the causes of the Georgian worldview. He proposes that the "Georgian" individual was created through the segmentation of time, of work from domestic life, of space, and of social position through adherence to particular rules of behavior. The separation of people from each other and the segmentation of their work support part of the social relationship necessary for capitalism to develop and thrive.

A trio of archaeologists who worked in the Archaeology in Annapolis project—Paul Shackel, Paul Mullins, and Mark Warner (1998:xvi)—summarize the core of its purpose: "Instead of accepting capitalism as a self-evident socioeconomic system or simply probing *how* capitalism has worked, Archaeology in Annapolis has attempted to confront *why* capitalism works, to identify the ways it breaks down, and to illuminate how class relationships are negotiated, contested, and resisted through material culture." The purpose of the work as a form of applied archaeology, useful to the wider public, has been to expose the origins of modern life and to demonstrate that our current culture and society are neither inevitable nor embedded in some unchanging human nature. The project's influential public program was designed to share that insight with thousands of visitors to open sites under excavation in the downtown area of the city.

The archaeologists in Annapolis have investigated dozens of sites in the city to "probe how apparent everyday minutia, such as food, gardens, architecture, and tablewares, have been significant mechanisms which have reproduced, modified, and resisted capitalist society over three hundred years" (Shackel et al. 1998:xv). In my own work in the Annapolis project, I have been most concerned with the ways that gender ideology became an essential element in the development of capitalism. Industrial capitalism, and indeed the whole culture of capitalism, relied upon a rigid distinction between domestic labor and labor in the workplace. Eighteenth-century gender ideology relied on religious authority, scientific authority, and natural law. Both custom and the legal code enforced the ideology.

Let me turn to the archaeology of an admirable 18th-century woman: Anne Catharine Green. She provides an example of the roles and limited options available to Euro-American women in the 18th century, but she is unusual in that some of her choices and actions as an individual can be identified in the archaeological record. She was a member of a gender whose power and voice were muted in a society where women had little autonomy. Each of her many roles, as daughter, wife, mother, mother-in-law, businesswoman, landowner, printer, patriot, and "relict" (widow), was wholly or partially defined and structured by gender.

In 1738, Anne Catharine Hoof and Jonas Green were married in Philadelphia. Jonas, one son of a long family line of printers, had worked for Benjamin Franklin, who may have arranged for Jonas' official appointment in the Maryland capital as printer to the province. The Greens moved to Annapolis and started a family and a business. Until her husband's death in 1767, Anne Catharine Green managed a household that consisted of children, servants, apprentices, employees, and, rarely, an enslaved domestic worker. She provided the household support necessary for her husband's social and political successes, and she almost certainly worked in the print shop as well. Anne Catharine took over the printing business and continued to manage the household when Jonas died. The General Assembly of Maryland awarded her the same terms of payment that her husband had received and appointed her to the official position of printer to the province. Until her death in 1775, Anne Catharine printed under her own name, as well as with her son William and later her son Frederick.

Not a great deal of historical documentation explicitly concerns the lives of middle-class and working-class women in the Chesapeake. Anne Catharine Green, however, is visible in the products of her press, such as official documents and the colonial newspaper. She appears intermittently in official documents and the probate inventory (list of possessions of a deceased person) of her estate survives.

The material culture most clearly associated with her consists of the imprints she produced and the possessions listed at probate. Although the archaeological assemblage represents an entire household made up of individuals of different gender and age, certain aspects of the record can be directly attributed to the short period of time when Anne Catharine was head of household.

Probate inventories can be read as descriptions of the interiors of houses and not merely as random lists of what people owned when they died. Because they are taken for specific individuals, they are one source of data that specifically associate material culture with gender. As one might expect, the items in the probate inventories of Jonas Green in 1767 and of Anne Catharine Green in 1775 are largely the same. Anne Catharine has some items Jonas does not, but fewer items overall. The point in comparing inventories, then, is not to identify particular items with the gender of the head of household. Instead, I want to raise a question about the organization of the items within the house and shop. I suggest that while Jonas was alive material was organized in a way we would recognize as more "orderly" in the Georgian sense. Anne Catharine rearranged material to reflect a different set of values, one in which domestic labor and craft labor were not entirely separated.

Comparing her inventory with that of her husband suggests that Anne Catharine was less concerned with separating domestic life from business life. While Jonas apparently kept all printing and bookbinding material in the shop and kept a separate office for himself, Anne Catharine rearranged the printing material, keeping paper and tools in the house rather than in the shop. She moved the eight-day clock out of the print shop. The probate takers listed a bookstand, printing paper, and some imprints among kitchenwares and ceramics. The bookbinders press had been moved out of the shop and into the house. I believe that a domestic-focused task orientation, rather than a wage/labor time orientation, guided Anne Catharine's workplaces.

The building sequence of the Greens' house and shop also indicates a changing configuration of space and suggests that while Anne Catharine was head of household she rearranged more than objects. While Jonas was alive the house and shop were remodeled several times. By his death in 1767 the house stood apart from the print shop. Jonas wrote that the shop was completely unconnected to the house in the *Maryland Gazette* (Dec. 12, 1756), trying to allay fears of contagion during a smallpox epidemic after one of his children died of the disease. During her tenure as head of household from 1767 to 1775, Anne Catharine built a rather wide hyphen with its own fireplace to connect the southern L of the house with the shop. Later, their son Frederick removed the hyphen so that the house and the shop were again separate buildings. Thus, Anne Catharine, in contrast to her husband and probably her son, chose literally to reconnect the domestic and work domains.

Does this mean that Anne Catharine represents some sort of nonmodern thinking during the time when Anglo-American life was shifting and changing to an individual-based culture? I think it really means that our research and our questions need to be continually complicated by reality. Historical archaeology is a challenging practice. It is so tempting to come up with easy material culture "tests" of particular ideas and then confirm what we already think we know. Remember the discussion about acculturation, with which archaeologists boxed themselves into biased assumptions and results? Think also about the ambiguity of our evidence (both material and documentary). Anne Catharine reminds us that there is never just one story, even within what looks like one culture.

CHAPTER 19

Australia's Convict Past

And I'm gone on the rising tide
For to face Van Diemen's land

—U2

In the liner notes to the album *Rattle and Hum*, the band U2 dedicates the song "Van Diemen's Land" to John Boyle O'Reilly. O'Reilly's life took him from his native Ireland to England, Australia, and the United States, demonstrating some of the global connections of the 19th century. Arrested in England for high treason for his Fenian (Irish nationalist) activities, his death sentence was commuted to penal servitude and he was transported to Australia, where he arrived in 1868. He escaped on the New Bedford whaling ship the *Gazelle* and sailed to America in 1869. O'Reilly became an energetic and respected leader in the Irish community in Boston's Back Bay and edited the *Pilot* newspaper until his death in 1890. His importance to the community is reflected in the memorial monument by the sculptor Daniel Charles French, dedicated in 1896, and in annual commemorations in the city.

O'Reilly holds some fascination in Australia as well. The Premier of Western Australia spoke at a John Boyle O'Reilly Commemoration ceremony in 2001, referring to the creation of an interpretive center at Australind to educate both residents and visitors about "this remarkable Irishman." Geoff Gallop stated:

Indeed in many ways, John Boyle O'Reilly epitomized what many Australians regard as our Irish inheritance; a lack of respect for undemocratic authority, a belief in equality, and a right to justice. Although we sometimes fall short of the mark, it pleases me to say that Australians have great tolerance and respect for each other, borne out of our rich multicultural heritage. I would hope that if John Boyle O'Reilly were to set foot on our shores today, he would find, if not in climate, at least in the hearts of her people, a less harsh and unfamiliar temperament. (2001)

I start with this quick look at O'Reilly because of his enduring memory, his cross-continental importance, his legacy as a champion of the oppressed, and his convict experience. As far as I know there is no archaeology associated with O'Reilly or with the sites of his incarceration. However, there is a growing and vibrant archaeology of the convict experience across Australia.

Van Diemen's Land, which is Tasmania, is quite a distance from Western Australia, where O'Reilly was sent. Australia's convict-era heritage covers the continent and includes places of convict incarceration such as jails, labor factories, prison farms, and internment camps. The infamous Port Arthur in Tasmania is now a historic site and tourism destination. Among other places recognized as part of the country's convict heritage are First Government House and the Great Northern Road, both of which were built with convict labor.

Britain commenced the colonization of Australia in 1788 by establishing the convict colony of New South Wales. As we saw in the chapter on the enclosure of the English countryside, major social changes and population movements resulting from land enclosures and the industrial revolution produced an increase in the landless and laboring poor. Arguments about what to do with such populations culminated in the decision to remove a whole range of people, from violent criminals to petty offenders, from the British Isles and sentence them to penal servitude and permanent exile in a new colony on the other side of the globe. The last convicts arrived in 1868 in Western Australia, placing O'Reilly at the end of an 80-year experiment.

Of the 74,000 convicts transported to Van Diemen's Land between 1803 and 1854, 12,000 were women, many of whom had been convicted of petty domestic theft. Upon arriving in Australia, each woman was assigned to the "crime class" at one of the female factories (women's prisons modeled after English workhouses) for at least six months. There she was to reform herself through both work—such as sewing, laundry, and textile production—and prayer. If she successfully served this probationary period, she moved into the "hiring class" and became eligible to finish her sentence as an unpaid domestic servant for a free colonist. If a woman became perceived as a disciplinary problem she would be moved into the "punishment class" and sentenced to periods in solitary confinement.

In operation from 1848 to 1854, the Ross Female Factory was adapted in 1847 from an earlier Road Gang Station built for male convicts. It is the most archaeologically intact female convict site in Australia. Today, the historic site is managed by the Parks and Wildlife Service of Tasmania and the Tasmanian Wool Centre of Ross. Eleanor Casella has worked there with community volunteers, regional and avocational archaeologists, local schoolteachers, Aboriginal Heritage Officers, and university students. She excavated to compare daily life among the crime, punishment, and hiring classes and also to compare these with life at the assistant superintendent's quarters. Some particularly interesting results pertain to the solitary cells endured by those in the punishment class.

Historic documents about the renovation of the Road Gang Station into the Female Factory indicate that floorboards were installed into the convict dormitories as part of the renovation. Luckily for the archaeologist, this modification ensures that all of the artifacts recovered from deposits that were under the floorboards relate directly to the female convicts rather than to the earlier male convicts. In the crime class areas, these artifacts include clues to forbidden activities, as there were alcohol bottle fragments and kaolin tobacco pipes, indicating drinking and smoking. While incarcerated, women were dependent on provisions provided by the Convict Department, but the archaeology suggests that surreptitious trade networks smuggled illicit tobacco, alcohol, and food.

Most of the ceramic and glass artifacts recovered from both the hiring and crime class dormitories were small fragments of cheap, mass-produced plates, cups, and bottles. Not surprisingly, the artifacts recovered in the assistant superintendent's quarters indicate greater access to higher quality goods. Household items there included colorful transfer-printed crockery and decorated drinking glasses.

The solitary cells are the only remaining separate treatment cells built explicitly for punishment of female convicts and as such they are considered highly significant for Australia's convict heritage. These cells were designed to maximize isolation. Rough-cut sandstone walls, approximately 20 inches thick, minimized sound transfer and therefore any communication between cells. Excavations revealed individual cells just large enough to accommodate a single inmate at roughly 4 by 6 feet.

Unlike the crime and hired-class dormitories, floors in the solitary cells were of packed earth. The floors were significantly lower than the cell doors, suggesting that entry required a descent into the cramped, darkened, silent cell for up to three weeks of isolation and decreased food rations. Archaeological deposits indicate that convicts tried to lessen the degradation and isolation of such solitary confinement through forbidden items. Archaeologists recovered evidence of tobacco, alcohol, and increased food rations in each excavated cell.

Some time after 1851 a fire, concentrated in the southern half of one cell, affected at least the two adjoining cells. Eleanor Casella interprets the fire as arson, drawing on documents from other female factories that suggest convicts committed arson to create public spectacles and call public attention to the violence they encountered in confrontations with guards. The Ross Factory authorities restored the structure and relaid the floors of the solitary cells with a second layer of hard earth. These new earthen floors were less easily adapted, and more easily inspected, for caches of forbidden materials. The new floors were partially successful, as the frequency of "luxuries" in the solitary cells decreased. However, they did not disappear. The material remains of the forbidden activities were both scattered through the new floor and concentrated inside a small pit dug within the western cell.

Of course, incarceration is not the end of the convict story. Convicts were treated according to a graded system depending on their crimes, behavior, skill, and education. One could move up, toward freedom, or down, toward a penal settlement or the gallows. Many convicts were farmed out as assigned servants to farms or businesses run by free settlers or former convicts. These "employers" are another part of the story. Graham Connah calls attention to the role of assigned servants in the creation of privilege and the elite status of free settlers in his study of Archibald Clunes Innes and the Lake Innes Estate, now managed by the New South Wales National Parks and Wildlife Service as part of the Lake Innes Nature Reserve.

Innes was typical of early 19th-century free settlers from the middle and upper classes in Britain, in that he had poor prospects at home and was looking for economic opportunities. He arrived in Sydney in 1822 as an army officer and ended up with a land grant in the Port Macquarie area of New South Wales where he moved with his wife in 1831. He had high ambitions. Connah (2001:141) writes, "He appears to have seen himself as a Scots laird of the developing area....He even had his personal piper, so that the skirl of bagpipes could remind everyone of who he was....He saw himself as part of an emerging Australian aristocracy."

Excavations at his estate revealed an expansive and expensive way of life. For example, Connah is amazed at the complexity of the plumbing of this early frontier property, including elaborately decorated toilets crafted by the Wedgwood factory in England. Such luxury was based not on wealth but on the unpaid labor of an extraordinary number of skilled individuals. In 1837 there were 91 assigned servants working for Innes and his wife. In addition, there may have been wage laborers as well, so it is difficult to tease apart servant quarters of convict laborers from those of free laborers. Excavation of a structure in the damp, low-lying servants' village reveals evidence of wooden buildings with earthen floors and brick fireplaces but apparently without window glass. The thin scatter of artifacts testifies to the material poverty of life at the bottom of the socioeconomic ladder.

Innes and others with similar ambitions failed to create an Australian aristocracy with their privilege supported by others' servitude. When his access to free labor dried up, Innes was financially ruined and had to take paid employment to support himself and his family. The idea of an Australian aristocracy failed to achieve official recognition and the transport of convicts eventually ceased.

The memory and meaning of the convict past, however, persists in both Australia and Ireland, where historic jails are preserved to commemorate the shared heritage of British exile. Casella has visited such places in both countries. She summarizes the different but connected meanings they have:

> Australian heritage gaols can be read as commemorations of "belonging"—of forging a new nation, of fermenting a non-European and distinctly *Australian* consciousness. In contrast, Irish gaol museums commemorate a heritage of "longing"—of yearning for those absent relatives, of tracing the missing generations through their antipodean accomplishments. (2005:464)

Casella's observation highlights the cultural importance of historical migrations from Ireland to Australia. Such distinctly different ways of conceptualizing connections and loyalties are important features of the stories of massive migrations throughout the development of the modern world. Ties between nations of origin and colonies can become complicated, particularly when migrants are unwilling (and are more accurately termed captives) and when prejudice affects life in the new homeland. In the next chapter, we look at a variety of sites associated with the African diaspora and in chapter 25 we look explicitly at some tangible connections between Africa and African Americans. In chapter 29, we again look at some connections between the Irish and Irish diasporic communities.

CHAPTER 20

African American Life

People are trapped in history and history is trapped in them.

—JAMES BALDWIN

The archaeology of African American life has become an essential and prominent part of historical archaeology since the 1970s. Because it is so important and varied, I decided against choosing one site to visit in this windshield survey. Instead, this is a tour within a tour. As the subfield developed, archaeologists often focused on plantation slavery but have expanded questions to consider the various roles and situations of black Americans as enslaved and free, rural and urban. Post–Civil War tenant plantations and southern farms and the lives of free blacks provide opportunities for theorizing, analyzing, and describing strategies of power, expressions of all levels of ideology, and dynamic interactions among those attempting to dominate and those attempting to resist. The archaeology of slavery provides evidence for a range of resistance, from covert slave resistance on plantations to the overt resistance of claiming one's own freedom through the Underground Railroad.

Theresa Singleton, one of the most well-known practitioners of African American archaeology, has dubbed its early development as "moral mission archaeology," due to its roots in the black activism of the civil rights movement. She offers this appreciative critique of the legacy of these beginnings:

Moral mission archaeology sought to interpret the everyday lives of African Americans from their own perspectives using the remains of housing, foodways, and personal effects recovered from excavations. It succeeded in giving a voice to the voiceless, but many of the interpretations were overly simplistic....Further, by choosing African survival rather than its demise or reconfiguration as a research focus, moral mission archaeology established a research precedent that still stalks African-American archaeology today: the search for cultural markers linked to Africa as the most significant aspect of African-American material life. (1999:2)

When Charles Fairbanks began his work at Florida's Kingsley Plantation in 1968, he consciously entered an ongoing anthropological and larger social debate about whether Africans could have retained any of their own culture after the horrors of the Middle Passage (that is, the transatlantic slave trade) and slavery. In spite of Carter G. Woodson's 1933 book, *The Mis-education of the Negro*, which reclaimed African American history, many histories of African American life continued to be subject to the denigrating "myth of the Negro past," which essentially denied history or culture to African Americans. It was this myth that anthropologist Melville Herskovits named and, joining African American scholars, sought to correct through his study of "Africanisms." Herskovits argued for a distinct African American culture. It was these African survivals, or Africanisms, that Fairbanks sought in the remains excavated from slave cabins. This beginning is what Singleton sees as somewhat simplistic, but it was an important step, as Fairbanks' work initiated the archaeology of African American life.

Although many studies have focused largely on plantation life in the southern United States, the context of enslavement was pervasive, extending far beyond such settings to small farms, urban homes, artisans' shops, industries, docks, and other places throughout the New World. The "rediscovery" of slavery in New York City due to the uncovering of the African Burial Ground in lower Manhattan came as a surprise to many. However, slavery was part of everyday life in the northern United States as well as in the South. Emancipation occurred in different years in the northern and southern states. The aftermath of continued racism, constructed to justify slavery and disenfranchisement, has persisted everywhere that slavery was practiced.

There is currently a movement within historical archaeology to broaden the context of research by considering the African diaspora as a whole. This broadening provides a global perspective over an extended time period and considers how the diaspora is intertwined with the widespread phenomena of colonialism, imperialism, and emerging capitalism. For example, within the period of enslavement, this broad approach can compare the lives and strategies of Africans throughout the Americas, under different colonial regimes (such as the Dutch, English, French, Portuguese, and Spanish), and in various relationships with Native peoples. Historical archaeologists seek to understand the influences of African cultures and to examine how African American culture derived from African heritage. This search makes use of the concepts of creolization and the dynamism of meanings that people assign to material culture to make sense of this complicated history. The questions are compelling: How does a distinct cultural identity get expressed? How can it be interpreted through archaeology? Is there evidence for resistance to imposed identity and behavior? How were cultural boundaries created and maintained?

Some of the evidence with which such questions have been addressed include the rather plain but very important category of ceramics known as earthenwares. Colonoware is a coarse earthenware that was locally made and has been found in colonized North America in the Chesapeake region, South Carolina, and the Caribbean. When first identified, it was dubbed colono-Indian ware to distinguish it as a contact-period ceramic made by Native Americans. This unique material culture expression has become an important focus of research, figuring in discussions about African Americans, Native Americans, creolization, and the creation of the color line. Archaeologists hotly debate its makers, users, and meanings. Leland Ferguson challenges the long-standing assumption that colonoware was solely a Native American product. In analyzing cultural interactions among African Americans, Native Americans, and European Americans, he demonstrates that, in South Carolina, colonoware has a strong African American connection.

Ferguson interprets colonoware and associated foodways in South Carolina to trace a specifically African American cultural tradition in the American South. Colonoware makes up about 70 percent of ceramics recovered from slave quarters in South Carolina but only 2 percent from urban sites. These vessels made by enslaved women show very little evidence of group segmentation or hierarchy, as the pottery is very similar from site to site. It is plain and undecorated and is similar to contemporary pottery of West Africa. Cooking jars and a high frequency of bowls suggest a West African style of cooking and eating. In Africa, such ceramics were used to prepare and serve a kind of stew made of starch (millet, rice, or maize) with some vegetable relish and some meat or fish. A person would eat simply with the hands, taking some starch and dipping or scooping the other food in the bowl. Ferguson emphasizes the maintenance of rural folk culture, observing that enslaved African Americans on the rice plantations of South Carolina "were within an ethnic environment that must have emphasized reciprocal relationships with one another, resourcefulness, competence and traditional ties to ancestral culture" (Ferguson 1991:37).

Like colonoware, "Chesapeake pipes" are made from local clays and are found dating to contexts from the 1630s to the 1730s. Such pipes excavated from Flowerdew Hundred plantation on the James River in Virginia have become another major source of controversy. Some archaeologists analyze these pipes and compare them with African examples, concluding that bowl forms, techniques, and decorative motifs point to African styles and therefore African American rather than European American or Native American manufacture. These interpretations are fiercely contested by other archaeologists, who are convinced that the Chesapeake pipes and colonoware are more likely made by Native Americans. A group of archaeologists working in the Chesapeake protest that historical archaeologists often overlook the role of Native Americans in colonial times. They rightly emphasize that Native Americans remained a viable presence in the colonies and did not disappear, as so many versions of history imply. They raise an important point about the questions being asked and suggest that trying to identify specific makers of locally made earthenwares may be asking the wrong question altogether. Specifically, these archaeologists wonder if archaeologists should even attempt to assign modern ethnic categories to the makers of artifacts in a Creole society like the 17th-century Chesapeake.

Although much archaeological research on African American history focuses on the context of enslavement, there is obviously much more to the story. Enslaved people sometimes gained their freedom. Some were emancipated; some emancipated themselves, "stealing" themselves away to fugitive Maroon communities or to free states or other countries. The study of Maroon communities (settlements established by fugitives) contributes to themes of the African diaspora in the Americas and is particularly important for understanding the effects of cultural contact, shifting alliances, and the complexities of life in marginal areas. Archaeologists have investigated such Maroon settlements to varying degrees. These include Nannytown, Accompong, and Seaman's Valley in Jamaica; Jose Leta in the Dominican Republic, Culpepper Island in North Carolina; and Pilaklikaha and Fort Mose in Florida.

The unusually large and long-lived kingdom of Palmares in Brazil is an extraordinary example of a Maroon settlement. Palmares (the name means "palm groves" in Portuguese) lasted from 1605 to 1694, situated inland from the plantations along the east coast of Brazil in hilly forested areas. It was established by fugitive slaves fleeing sugar plantations, but the population grew steadily to include self-liberated Africans, native Brazilian Indians, and some outcast Europeans. Because it was described by the Europeans who attacked it, we know some basic information from the documentary record, although the point of view in such records nearly guarantees biased reporting. In 1645 a Dutch lieutenant described one of at least two substantial towns as the seat of the king. This capital contained 220 houses, a church, four forges, and a large council house. By 1677 there were 10 major towns and several smaller outposts. At its maximum size, Palmares was home to approximately 20,000 inhabitants.

Charles Orser and Pedro Funari have identified and investigated several sites in the capital of Macaco, also known as Serra da Barriga (Potbelly Hill). The continuous state of warfare that the fugitive settlement lived under affected the location of the settlements and daily life. For example, all of the sites are located strategically in relation to the River Mundau, which colonial troops traveled on when they attacked, as they did frequently.

Archaeological research finds that these runaway people did not live in isolation. The towns were well fortified and the residents grew crops, fished, and traded with local tribes and even Portuguese colonists who flouted the colonial government's prohibitions against trade with the fugitives. Much of the archaeological evidence consists of three different categories of ceramics: glazed European, unglazed Native, and glazed locally made. The European wares are Portuguese and Dutch, indicating trading between the Maroons and nonelite colonists. The Tupinamba Native-style vessels may have been made by Native Brazilian women married to Maroons. The local wares are wheel-thrown and are, so far as known, unique to Palmares. These coarse earthenwares are made in a style that blends indigenous and African elements.

Palmares was a long-lived Maroon settlement that became a powerful threat to Portuguese and Dutch colonial powers in Brazil. The Portuguese attacked the city for decades, finally destroying it and executing its leaders, including the famous King Zumbi. With the restoration of national civilian rule in the 1980s, Serra da Barriga was declared a National Heritage Monument. Palmares is an important national place. Its history and meaning are focal points of discussion about black consciousness and working for a more democratic and less racist Brazilian society.

Another Maroon settlement, Gracia Real de Santa Teresa de Mose, created in 1738, was the first legally sanctioned free black town in the United States. The Spanish established Fort Mose north of St. Augustine for those fleeing British slavery. In 1693, when the Spanish Crown declared that all fugitives would be given their freedom, captives in Carolina took advantage of this sanctuary policy. Africans manipulated the Anglo-Spanish conflict over the lands between St. Augustine and Charleston, South Carolina, and got their own town in return for defense against the British. The African-Spanish settlement ended in 1763, when blacks evacuated with the Spanish to Cuba.

It became important for the initial investigations of Fort Mose to identify and verify the site and its physical setting simply to affirm its reality. The investigators—an archaeologist and a historian—remark on the local struggle over the research project: "It is evident, however, that the idea that free African Americans made important contributions to the defense and culture of St. Augustine is an unfamiliar and difficult concept for many residents, for whom slavery remains the dominant (if not exclusive) paradigm for black history" (Deagan and Landers 1999:263).

It is indeed difficult for many people to become familiar with a legacy of free black life because traces on the landscape—whole towns—have been

FIGURE 7. This cellar on the site of New Philadelphia, Illinois, is from a home built in the 1850s. Tax records indicate that Sarah McWorter, daughter of Frank and Lucy McWorter, destroyed the building in 1868. The cellar was filled with domestic refuse such as ceramics and animal bone and also with destruction rubble, including wall plaster. This structure appears to have been framed and sided with clapboard. (*Courtesy of Paul A. Shackel*)

erased from memory. I mention four very different places—Seneca Village in New York City, New Philadelphia in Illinois, Freedman's Town in Houston, and Ransom Place in Indianapolis—to illustrate a concerted effort to regain that history.

With cooperation and assistance of the descendant community, Diana diZerega Wall and Nan Rothschild are investigating Seneca Village, a neighborhood of African American landowners and Irish immigrants. The community lasted only a few decades from the 1820s to the 1850s, when the city took the land by eminent domain to create Central Park. The project participants hope to reintroduce this early history into New York's perception of its past.

At the site of New Philadelphia in west-central Illinois, archaeologists are asking questions about life in a biracial community on the western frontier before and after the Civil War. The town was established by an African American, "Free Frank" McWorter, in 1836. McWorter had purchased his own

FIGURE 8. This is the same McWorter cellar shown in figure 7, but photographed to give a sense of the landscape. You can get a sense of how invisible even substantial archaeological features are to the above-ground observer. (*Courtesy of Paul A. Shackel*)

freedom with money he earned in the saltpeter mines of Kentucky. After moving to Illinois, he subdivided 42 acres to form the town and then used what he earned from the sale of the lots to purchase the freedom of family members. McWorter was not only the town founder, but also proprietor, promoter, and developer. African Americans as well as those of European descent moved to New Philadelphia. The town reached its peak after the Civil War with a population of about 170, comparable in size to many towns in the vicinity today. The town's death knell was sounded when the railroad was engineered to avoid it and, by the early 1900s, only a few families remained. By 1940 the area of the town was used only for farming. The local community instigated the New Philadelphia project, which continues to build relationships with the town's descendants, some of whom are local and many of whom are broadly dispersed. The project aims to understand how people created and maintained this integrated community and how it disintegrated during the Jim Crow era.

After the end of the Civil War in 1865, freed African Americans were drawn to Houston to make new lives. They reclaimed land from the swampy and flood-prone area south of the Buffalo Bayou and built a community. By the end of the 1800s, Freedman's Town was the prosperous and successful center of black Houston. Over 500 structures were standing when the town was listed in the National Register of Historic Places as a historic district. Today, 20 years later, largely due to gentrification, fewer than 30 structures remain. The Rutherford B. H. Yates Museum sponsors the Yates Community Archaeology Program (YCAP). YCAP aims to reclaim and tell this history through oral histories; archaeological research; historic preservation; and partnerships with schools, universities, churches, and other organizations to create opportunities for education.

In Indiana in the 1960s, members of the local African American community were displaced when their neighborhood was razed as a slum to make way for the expansion of Indiana University–Purdue University Indianapolis. Much of the cleared land simply became parking lots, a fate that preserved much of the extensive archaeological record. The Ransom Place Project combines oral history and archaeology to reclaim the history of this erased neighborhood. Project director Paul Mullins summarizes the implications of the landscape for reinforcing or challenging perceptions:

> Once a space in which state power, student privileges and neighborhood rights clashed along the color line, today the landscape is a remarkably uncontested sea of parking lots and institutional architecture. The discord over campus park-

ing is superficially mundane and may seem rather disconnected to racism, yet it is symptomatic of how the landscapes of urban renewal have effaced heritage, eluded race and allowed many people to ignore how their privileges were historically secured along color and class lines. (2006:61)

Archaeologists have successfully brought a measure of complexity and sophistication to their questions and approaches about African American archaeology. They also have come to appreciate the value that involvement of descendant communities can bring to the methods, results, and meaning of the work. We'll see more of this intense descendant interest in several of the chapters in the section on public scholarship.

CHAPTER 21

The Machine in the Garden

Men make their own history, but they do not make it just as they please; they do not make it under circumstances chosen by themselves, but under circumstances directly found, given and transmitted from the past. The tradition of all the dead generations weighs like a nightmare on the brain of the living.
—KARL MARX

While manufacturing and iron production began in England's American colonies during the 17th century and crafts began to turn into industries in the 18th century, it is during the 19th century when full-blown industry and accompanying commerce appeared, just slightly behind the industrial revolution in England. Industry changed the structure of wage labor, yet slave labor continued in agricultural, industrial, commercial, and domestic settings. The economy of the United States continued to change after the upheavals of the Civil War and Reconstruction and with the impact of the Depression of the 1930s. Immigration, anti-immigration laws, and internal migration continued to affect the makeup of the population.

Harpers Ferry sits at the confluence of the Shenandoah and Potomac Rivers in the Blue Ridge Mountains of West Virginia. The area is prone to severe flooding. The floods leave behind thick deposits of silt that can be dated precisely using the date of the flood. In that way, the floods have been good for dating archaeological deposits. However, they were not good for communities or industries. In spite of the constant threat of floods, President George Washington insisted that Harpers Ferry be the location of one of the new national armories (the other was established in Springfield, Massachusetts).

As one of the most significant early industrial communities in the United States, Harpers Ferry provides an extraordinarily rich archaeological record of the ways that changing industrial practices affected—and continue to

FIGURE 9. This profile of an excavation unit at Harpers Ferry National Historical Park shows the deep flood deposits that separate and help to assign dates to layers of archaeological deposits. (*Courtesy Paul A. Shackel*)

affect—domestic life and social relations. From the establishment of the United States Armory in 1796 to the establishment of the National Park, "industry displaced craft, craftsmen revolted, entrepreneurs developed new industrial surveillance technologies to control workers, and nineteenth- and twentieth-century citizens commemorated the glories and success of the industrial revolution" (Shackel 1996:3).

Before I delve into a story of archaeology at Harpers Ferry, I need to digress a bit and provide some context with which to better understand it. Two truths about the human condition help us understand the importance of both culture and history. As quoted above, Marx observed that we make our own history, subject to the conditions we inherit. However, those conditions are more than physical. It is also true, as Elizabeth Brumfiel explains (2003:217), that "humans dwell in a reality that is both material and ideal; that is, humans live in a physical world, but a physical world that they comprehend only through their own constructed models." Because people do not live only in the world, but also live "in their heads," cultural metaphors are a very useful organizing principle for framing questions about people's lives.

How do people maintain and change their understandings, interpretations, and images within a changing world? We use both textual and nontextual material culture as well as speech, performance, and other nonmaterial mental practices to create settings in which we structure understandings of our lives. Practitioners of cognitive semantics see metaphor as a basic cognitive function of the human mind. They explain metaphor as a kind of cognitive mapping that has its source in the experienced world and its expression in language. A root metaphor is an underlying association, which may or may not be explicitly obvious to individuals who use it to shape their understandings.

Cognitive linguists George Lakoff and Mark Johnson find the basis of metaphor in physical experience, that is, in one's sense and image of one's own body. In addition, I believe that people create understandings from the spatial and material contexts of their experiences. Lakoff grounds metaphor in day-to-day bodily experience, but it is crucial to understand that such experience is not "natural" in any noncultural sense; nor is it expressed in language only. It is expressed, clarified, and worked out in material culture as well. Therefore, material culture, not just the human body, is a source for language. Material culture may also be used, like language, to express multi-layered cultural metaphors.

During the late 18th and early 19th century, debates about the merits of agrarian versus industrial economy confronted the new American nation with choices about its identity and relationship with the rest of the world. Americans were wary of the new industrial technology, concerned that the appalling conditions of England's industrial revolution would be created at home. Thomas Jefferson and Benjamin Franklin promoted agrarianism, but Alexander Hamilton and Tench Coxe argued for industrialism and the need for manufacturing, believing that the country's political independence rested on economic independence.

Pro-agrarians believed that industry would destroy the moral fiber of society. Pro-industrialists initially made some concessions by attempting to make industry subservient and secondary to agriculture, for example by placing factories in pastoral landscapes rather than in cities. The history of rural industry is much less familiar to most Americans than the urban factory. It is, however, an important chapter in the nation's economic and social history.

If the garden of the New World as a kind of promised land was a root metaphor during the 18th century in America, it was challenged as the metaphor of the machine infiltrated and become a dominant cultural symbol. Changes wrought by the "machine in the garden" were the changes of the industrializing society. The machine that invaded the New World garden was not just new technology, but a wholly different metaphor for organizing and comprehending daily life. To understand such change requires paying attention to all of the forms of material and textual expression that 18th- and 19th-century people used.

Paul Shackel is interested in how the inhabitants of Harpers Ferry tried to reconcile the conflict between the garden and the machine—that is, between competing cultural metaphors and ways of life—and how workers coped with deskilling and loss of their craft to mechanization. He examines life in the town through an investigation of two sites. One site was home to the households of successive master armorers, who were in charge of the daily management of the factory. These occupations date from 1821 to 1830 and from 1830 to 1850. Another site was home to armory workers and their families. Pieceworkers lived there from 1821 to 1841, and then mechanics and wage laborers occupied the home from 1841 to 1852.

Analysis of botanical remains, including macroflora (visible plant remains), pollen, and phytoliths (microscopic mineral particles that form in plants), shows how workers used the yards around their homes and how the armory grounds were kept. The changes in landscapes reflect the effects of town development, commerce, concerns about health in low-lying swampy areas, industry, and the persistence of a craft ethos. There are noticeable differences between the landscape of the first quarter of the 19th century, when armorers subscribed to a craft ethos, and the second quarter of the 19th century, when industrial manufacturing became routine. Armory officials provided well-groomed and manicured lawns in the industrial environment until the 1830s, when industrial work processes were established. After that time, pollen and phytolith analysis suggest that weedy plants took over. By the 1840s the military had taken control of the armory and began to standardize the landscape by grading; constructing new, orderly factory buildings; and creating a grid pattern for the town.

Archaeology also shows people's responses to changes in industry as the armory was transformed from a workplace run by artisans to a factory of wage laborers run by the military. Shackel suggests some of the factors that motivate individuals to adopt new purchasing patterns:

The deskilling of workers and the embracing of the material world associated with wage labor were not acceptable to some employees. While there were relatively few explicit protests, such as strikes, at Harpers Ferry, workers did rebel by slowing production, by damaging equipment, and by frequent absenteeism. In the domestic sphere, some families chose alternative goods for the types of material culture they acquired. These goods were not the goods that were often purchased by those conforming to the ideology of mass production and mass consumption. Consumers... were often middle-class women who were making choices about what types of goods they should purchase. These decisions demonstrated their commitment or their lack of commitment to the new consumer culture and the Romantic ideal. Acquiring out-of-date materials that were fashionable generations earlier may possibly show consumers' discontent for the new modern culture. (1996:145)

Workers were not silent about their disintegrating social and economic position. Reactions on the job to harsher work conditions and longer hours included work slowdowns, sabotage and, in one extreme case, the harassment and murder of armory superintendent Thomas Dunn. As Shackel observes, families also made different consumer choices in this chaotic environment. During the early 19th century, when the lives and livelihoods of craftsmen appeared unthreatened and secure, the households of management and labor tended to follow the same fashions in choosing their domestic goods. Later, in mid-century, the managers continued to adopt new styles but, in contrast, laborers readopted old styles even while both cost and availability made the new and fashionable household goods accessible to the average armory worker.

In short, findings at Harpers Ferry are counterintuitive. So much for intuition! Our common assumptions lead us to believe that all people want new, fashionable goods for their homes, that all people participate in the marketplace in similar ways. In our marketing-obsessed, consumer society, we seem to be deeply convinced of this, but historical archaeology reveals time and time again that choices about consumption are motivated by many factors other than wealth or the passive willingness to buy as much of whatever new commodity is being marketed simply based on affordability.

The results of the archaeological research offer visitors to Harpers Ferry National Historical Park opportunities to experience evidence of cultural diversity and the consequences of history at this site and in the larger process of industrialization. As you enter the park's orientation exhibit, you may turn left or right. To the left are exhibit panels set inside the large portal from the famous Bollman Railroad Bridge. On one of these panels is the compelling statement that "America's first successful use of interchangeable parts took place in Harpers Ferry" (in the 1820s and 1830s). If you turn to the right, you'll find a series of displays that are set up as if you are looking into windows. The segment "Armory Workers at Home" explains that during the 1820s and 1830s workers at the armory brought guns and gun parts home to work on them. Archaeological excavations at armory workers' houses revealed the artifacts that suggest this practice. The excavated gun parts and tools are displayed with an explanation of what they indicate about work during the piecework era, before the military took over the armory and instituted a wage labor system. The excavated artifacts make the argument for this previously unknown work practice.

The broader context of the exhibit is the changing labor practices of industrialization and related social issues. One section highlights the ethnicity of immigrant workers by showing an excavated rosary, Home Rule pipe, and a holy water font attributed to Irish Catholics. Another highlights women as boardinghouse keepers in an overcrowded town. This section suggests the complicated balance in a woman's life between running a business, raising a family, and the demands of femininity with the display of sherds of plates from boardinghouse meals, a baby bottle, and a perfume bottle. A third section shows an impressive array of patent medicine bottles, connecting commercialized medicine and industry. The text reads, in part, "Workers coping with machinery-related injuries and unhealthy workshops probably relied heavily on self-treatment." In this section, working conditions, substance abuse, and alternative medicine are all issues that connect pre–Civil War Harpers Ferry with the visitor today. Such connections may help visitors see some of the issues involved in the development and dilemmas of modern life.

CHAPTER 22

The Inner-City Working Class

Our progress in degeneracy appears to me to be pretty rapid. As a nation we began by declaring that "all men are created equal." We now practically read it "all men are created equal, except Negroes." When the Know-Nothings get control, it will read "all men are created equal, except Negroes and foreigners, and Catholics." When it comes to this, I shall prefer emigrating to some country where they make no pretense of loving liberty—to Russia, for example, where despotism can be taken pure, and without the base alloy of hypocrisy.

—ABRAHAM LINCOLN

In the early 19th century the working poor in American cities tended to be the native-born of European and African descent. The mid-century flood of immigration, particularly of those fleeing the Irish famine, changed the makeup of the urban population. In reaction, some Americans embraced anti-Catholic and antiforeign sentiments and actions. The emergence of the Know-Nothing political party, decried by Lincoln in the quote above, was one response to the changes. In this chapter, we'll take another tour within a tour to visit several inner-city sites.

Part of the reaction to a neighborhood like Five Points in New York City was the creation of a mythology about the immorality of life in the slum, creating and perpetuating stereotypes of the urban poor. Rebecca Yamin is impressed by the narrative strength of slum stories, regardless of evidence to the contrary. In other words, stereotypes die hard. She comments (2001:1), "Contemporaries characterized the Five Points neighborhood as a slum, but the clustering of immigrant groups along street fronts and the struggle for respectability, no matter how difficult the physical circumstances, is reminiscent of many neighborhoods in the city today."

A large and productive archaeological project investigated this 19th-century working-class neighborhood in lower Manhattan. Between 1790 and 1890 Five Points (named for the intersection in the city's Sixth Ward) changed from an outlying industrial district to one of the most congested residential areas in New York. You can get a visual sense of the neighborhood from the 2002 movie *Gangs of New York*, but you won't get a realistic picture of daily life. The archaeology suggests that a mix of households occupied the neighborhood, displaying disparate lifestyles. Some households owned at least some material culture that was much like that of wealthier parts of the city, perhaps indicating adoption of Victorian values of consumerism.

Such archaeological findings suggest that the circumstances of notorious urban slums in New York may have been similar to those in Washington, D.C.; West Oakland, California; and others around the country and around the world. Urban archaeologists in Australia, for example, have investigated Melbourne's Little Lonsdale Street, or "Little Lon," which was also full of Irish immigrants. The Rocks Discovery Museum tells the archaeological and historical story of Sydney's "Rocks," long perceived as the "wicked waterfront." The District Six Museum in Cape Town, South Africa, displays some of the archaeological material from excavations in the Horstley Street neighborhood there.

FIGURE 10. These figurines are from a five-story brick tenement at 472 Pearl Street in the Five Points neighborhood in Manhattan. The figurines, probably English-made, were recovered from a large privy in the rear courtyard of the property in an archaeological context dating between 1854 and 1870. This was a period in the tenement's history when it was inhabited by all Irish immigrant families and boarders, with the exception of a single German family. (*Courtesy of the General Service Administration*)

During the late 19th and early 20th century, the Washington, D.C., social reformers intent on housing reform turned their attention to alley dwellings. Historian James Borchert is critical of the Washington reformers' documentation of poor living conditions, believing that middle-class reformers found only what they intended to find and overemphasized disorder and pathology in their reports. Instead, Borchert contends that alley dwellers—mainly African Americans and foreign-born immigrants—used their folk experience to create strategies for surviving urban life. African Americans had poured into the city during and after the Civil War, which came to an end in 1865 and abolished legal slavery. The rapid population explosion led to crowding through infilling of blocks with alleys and the rapid erection of substandard housing.

Archaeology suggests that alley residents in Washington in the 1880s were using at least some of the accoutrements of middle-class display. Even the alley reformers found variety and the unexpected in spite of themselves. One reformer reports:

> With all the notoriety, the alleys remain fundamentally unchanged; some of the homes are comfortable, some are fair and some are, to use an over-used adjective, "deplorable." The people who live there represent many different grades of culture; some are coarse migrants, some suspicious and bitter, and other gracious and poised. (Borchert 1982:67)

The reports of house interiors by alley reformers varied widely, but the condition of yards was universally described as "filled with uncollected garbage, rubbish and filth." Borchert confirmed such observations by analyzing contemporary photographs. "Junking" was a full-time occupation for some alley men and supplemented many families' incomes. Children junked too. Junking involves

> collecting of glass bottles and breaking them to be sold as broken glass by the hundreds of pounds; selling of old rags, paper, iron and tin, and any article of value which may be found among trash cans, or on the dumps.... Thus the disorder in the backyard was often the alley family's savings account and insurance policy. (Borchert 1982:96)

Alley residents participated wholly in consumer culture, sometimes through secondhand shopping and barter. The mass market of the late 19th and 20th centuries would have excluded whole segments of society were it not for the secondhand trade, which allowed cash-poor consumers to acquire higher-quality goods. Secondhand stores may have allowed barter in addition to cash sales. Junk stores were common in 19th- and early 20th-century American cities, but trade in secondhand goods is not well documented in the written record.

Alley residents continued various strategies of "making do," a practiced way of life. For example, people collected and used wild food, even in the city. Archaeological evidence for the edible weedy plants of amaranth, purslane, and cruciferae (akin to watercress) has been recovered from at least one alley site in Washington. One alley reformer described how resourceful people were in gathering edible wild plants for food from vacant lots and the riverbank. There was plenty of local wild food to be found. The Works Progress Administration's Federal Writers Project (1937:26) reported that "[m]arshes of wild rice extend over much of the Anacostia River estuary, and, along the lower Potomac, wild celery, Peltandra, and various waterweeds."

Oral histories collected in neighboring southern Maryland provide another complication in considering the lives of African Americans in Washington after emancipation. People moved frequently between the city and rural areas. One family recounts an ancestor who worked as a hod carrier in construction (hods are V-shaped troughs filled with brick or mortar) to earn enough cash to move back to Charles County and eventually buy farmland. Land ownership was an important goal for African Americans and there is good reason to expect that some proportion of alley dwellers in the city were not as interested in buying fashionable goods or clothing for "status display" in their temporary home. Instead they were interested in accumulating enough cash to fulfill their dreams outside of the city.

Like other urban areas, West Oakland in the late 19th century was socially mixed with European immigrants, mainly Irish, and native-born black and white living in the same neighborhoods. And, like many cities, the mainstream image of West Oakland in the late 19th and 20th century was that of a dangerous slum. The contemporary importance as well as the historical importance of such urban studies should be clear. In the case of West Oakland, the slum stereotype, 19th-century history, 1950s history, and a recent earthquake all come together in the story of a large archaeology project.

The Loma Prieta earthquake struck the San Francisco Bay Area on October 17, 1989, collapsing the Cypress Freeway in West Oakland and killing 42 people. When the Cypress Freeway was first built in the 1950s, its path split the predominantly African American community and uprooted 600 families and dozens of businesses. The tragedy of the collapse of the freeway actually created the potential for healing some of the earlier damage to the community. West Oakland residents were determined to prevent the mistakes of the past from being repeated. They insisted upon participating in the dialogue over how and where the freeway would be reconstructed.

An important and long-lasting part of mitigating the impacts of the freeway and freeway construction on local residents was to ensure that the community benefited in meaningful ways from the project. Negotiations among the California Department of Transportation (Caltrans), the City of Oakland, and West Oakland community groups over the project design led to a number of additional community benefits, one of which was a historical archaeology project. That project forged important links between the researchers and the local present-day community. Caltrans and Sonoma State University developed an archaeological project, excavating sites along the freeway right-of-way. Some of those sites were households of former African American railroad porters. After the excavations some of the archaeological material became part of a traveling exhibit on African American labor history in West Oakland. The Cypress Freeway replacement project has become an important model for cooperation between agencies and communities. The Federal Highway Administration includes it in an example of their environmental justice efforts and success.

Archaeological project directors Mary and Adrian Praetzellis explain their approach:

> We ask complex and open-ended questions: how useful are the conventional standards of social prominence, wealth, education, and "culture" by which the "aristocrats of color" have been defined . . .? Indeed, what did "high status" mean in West Oakland and how was it expressed? How did these expressions vary from either contemporary norms or modern interpretations, and how did they vary between classes and ethnic groups? (2004:316)

The archaeology provided context and rich texture to the history of West Oakland. Archaeological questions address the choices made by different households. Researchers were able to group and compare documented households according to wealth and occupation. Higher-income groups sort into two categories of professionals according to how wealthy they were. Some professionals were very wealthy and others were wealthier than laborers in the lower-income groups of skilled and unskilled laborers. Researchers were also able to identify households by ethnicity or race, by whether the household owned or rented, and by the overall quality of the houses.

Addressing questions of "who bought what" leads to both unsurprising and surprising findings. Wine and hard liquor each had symbolic meanings connected to class identity and ideas about sophistication. In West Oakland, members of the better-paid professions tended to drink wine, as opposed to hard liquor. Although that result seems unremarkable, finding out who bought expensive meat is more surprising. In spite of expectations to the contrary, there is no evidence that wealthier households used more expensive cuts of meat than poorer ones. In fact, none of the four groups consistently bought less or more expensive meat. The quality of housing was a much better predictor of meat cost than profession or ethnicity. Residents of the least expensive homes used the least expensive meat overall, but renters tended to buy more expensive meat than owners. In sum, food choice was more strongly related to a household's immediate standard of living, correlated with the quality of their house, than economic status measured by profession, income, or homeownership.

The archaeology also reveals other kinds of household decisions, including evidence for hunting, fishing, and gathering wild food, activities that bridged the economic gap for many families. The researchers didn't expect to find the evidence they did of practices at odds with the law. Raising livestock in the city limits and the dumping of trash were not legal, but were done. The question of who recycled bottles and who just threw them out points to some interesting results as well. In the West Oakland economy, junk dealers paid cash for whole bottles. Households identified in the "unskilled group" left a smaller proportion of whole bottles in their refuse than other groups, indicating that they were recycling. They were not, however, the only ones. The richest had similar habits, tending to recycle rather than throw out bottles. The middle groups just threw their bottles out.

In addition, African Americans in general ate more beef than native-born whites. Judging by the measure of variability of tablewares and correlating the finding of more types of tableware with more household participation in the idealized Victorian dining ritual, it seems that African American working-class households had more in common with the white middle class than with whites who were also working class.

Social reformers often were confused by what they misinterpreted as the irrational behaviors of the poor. West Oaklanders were not extravagant in their spending habits, but made rational decisions based on their circumstances, relationships, and aspirations. The project finds that the unskilled category of households bought expensive meats, complex table settings, and fancy parlor bric-a-brac. The Praetzellises surmise:

> As society at large promoted behavior suitable to one's class, variation from this pattern would be considered subversive.... Meat in general and beef in particular had symbolic significance for many Americans. More than mere nutrition, it represented their aspirations and serving it was a matter of pride. Specifically, we propose that beef was a symbol of success in late-19th-century America; consequently, those who were excluded from conventionally assigned measures of social approval—such as African Americans and the unskilled working-class—particularly desired and purchased it. (2004:322)

Historical archaeologists often field the question of whether their work is necessary. In other words, could the same interpretations be made without the benefit of excavated artifacts? The question can be responded to with another series of questions: Does it matter what people actually do as opposed to what other people say they do? Should we, as students of the human condition, care about the gap between what people do and what they themselves say they do, or say that they wish to do? Should we be interested in the actual material conditions of people's lives and how those conditions relate to social context, political power or powerlessness, and cultural survival?

Projects that investigate the lives of the inner cities prompt us to rethink accepted categories and relationships. Results confront and challenge assumptions derived from documentary history and from stereotypes fueled by prejudice. In particular, archaeology challenges accepted ideals of economic rationality, resistance to societal pressures and expectations, and the material and social/cultural conditions of areas labeled as slums. Such insights can only be gained through data on what households actually buy, acquire, destroy, and discard.

CHAPTER 23

Garbage and Garbage-in-Waiting

It takes very special qualities to devote one's life to problems with no attainable solutions and to poking around in dead people's garbage: Words like "masochistic," "nosy," and "completely batty" spring to mind.

—PAUL BAHN

What would archaeologist Paul Bahn say about poking around in living people's garbage? Archaeologists have not been content for our skills to be confined to the study of the past. One part of modern material culture studies is the study of modern refuse dubbed "garbology." William Rathje and his students started the Garbage Project in the 1970s to use archaeology to address contemporary concerns, such as questions important to modern waste management and sociology. Garbologists have succeeded in measuring diet and nutrition, assessing resource waste and proposing methods to minimize waste, evaluating household participation in recycling programs, identifying household-level sources of hazardous wastes, cross-validating census counts of minority populations, and providing base data for the design of new "environmentally friendly" packages.

The Garbage Project rests on the simple premise that if discards can provide important information about past societies, then they should also provide such information about societies today. For the first couple of decades of this ongoing project, researchers sampled and recorded household trash (always guarding the anonymity of the residents). More recently they've expanded their work to landfills and exploded common myths about our solid waste problem.

Studying fresh garbage from households is messy and smelly. The garbologist-archaeologists sort and record packaging, food, and other waste items into myriad categories, including separating "once-edible food" from "food preparation debris." They have compared their data with surveys that record household responses to questions about what they throw away.

Analysis reveals some basic patterns in people's actions and perceptions. First, what people do is not the same as what they say they do. People do not accurately report what food they waste, what they recycle, their hazardous wastes, or what they eat and drink. Interestingly enough, there are some regularities—or, as Rathje terms them, "syndromes"—in the ways that people misrepresent their own behavior. The "surrogate syndrome" refers to accuracy provided by someone other than the consumer. For example, drinkers underreport their alcohol consumption. However, nondrinkers in a household accurately report what the drinkers consume. The "good provider syndrome" refers to the tendency for adult women reporting for a household to overreport everything the household uses.

Second, people who respond to surveys report rational behavior, but their actual behavior appears to be irrational. For example, during the United States' nationwide beef shortage of 1973, consumers complained about the high cost of beef and yet discarded more edible beef waste than ever. The additional waste probably was due to people buying cheaper and unfamiliar cuts, perhaps not knowing how to best prepare them and disliking the result. More recently, in response to admonitions about healthy diets and the need to consume less fat from red meat, people did indeed cut and discard more fat from their beef. However, they also consumed more processed meat, like sausages and hot dogs, which of course contains more fat and is less healthy.

From 1987 to 1995 Garbage Project archaeologists studied 30 tons of deposits from 15 different landfills across North America. Conventional wisdom suggested what they would find, based on popular assumptions about waste and biodegradation. Predictions were that fast-food packaging and disposable diapers would predominate; instead these items made up only 2 percent of the volume. Surprisingly, items that had received little public attention turned out to take up a lot of space. Even though researchers tried to avoid drilling through debris from construction and demolition (because of the damage caused to their equipment), such debris made up 20 percent or more of the landfill volume. The largest category, however, was paper. Nearly half of all the landfill that researchers excavated, measured, sorted, and recorded consisted of newspapers, magazines, packaging, printouts, and phonebooks.

Since the studies, many communities with recycling programs have understood the need to keep paper out of landfills, as it doesn't biodegrade as well as hoped. One of the resulting recommendations for all of us is that we should buy goods and packaging with "post-consumer recycled" content.

One of the general findings of the Garbage Project, when the results of many years of research are considered, is a somewhat disturbing disconnection between what people think is happening and what is really happening. Rathje offers an important observation from his decades of research about apparent disinterest in the material realities of behavior. In spite of some behavioral changes in response to findings (like changing recycling programs for paper), he reports that many of the Garbage Project's studies have been ignored after the results are reported because the results do not match preconceptions or other interests. He has surmised from his experience, for example, that the alcohol industry really doesn't want to reveal the extent of alcoholism in the United States. He also is surprised at the apparent disinterest from the U.S. Department of Agriculture in real data on household nutrition.

Rathje (2001:68) remarks: "I used to believe that people intentionally 'lie' in interviews today—in the past in texts and monuments. Now, I wonder if the differences between mental and material realities are not mainly simple cases of people not mentally recognizing material realities and fooling themselves." Along with Rathje, many historical archaeologists have direct and often frustrating experience with people's separate realities of mental, behavioral, and material life. Many of us observe disjunctures between the relative meaning and authority granted to different kinds of evidence, as documents are often assumed to be true even when physical material evidence provided by archaeology contradicts it (not what we may hope for, given our legal system's emphasis on material evidence). The relationship among such different realities is, as Rathje explains, a very important question for behavioral science to address because "only when all of these realities are in sync with each other can people plan rational public policies and make rational personal decisions." In other words, we may not know what we think we know and those misperceptions hurt our ability to make rational choices with predictable results.

Faced with obvious and important gaps in our understanding, of course, we can try to learn more and gain some useful understanding. One of the ways we learn is to design research by coming up with questions and then figuring out what kinds of evidence are needed to begin to address them. Consumerism clearly is directly related to garbage; we might even think about the things we buy as pregarbage. In the remainder of this chapter, I simply want to direct you to some issues and questions to think about. They come from the work of Teresita Majewski and Michael Schiffer, who study consumerism to better understand our modern society. They identify the following series of issues and propose questions that highlight the present-day relevance of material culture studies.

Issue #1. Structural and behavioral aspects of the emergence, growth, and maintenance of consumer societies. What do we need to understand to address this issue? We need to understand economic structural factors; the legal system and its effects on producing, selling, and buying; and both written and unwritten social rules about appropriate ownership. We need to ask how an activity becomes consumerized. That is, how can an activity come to require a continual updating of the material culture that's perceived as necessary for the activity to continue? Consumer societies are resource and energy intensive, but how is the concept of sustainability coming into play? How have international aspects of manufacturing, marketing, and consumption reconfigured people's lives? What are the roles of huge corporations in these processes?

Issue #2. Effects of consumerism on the life histories of specific products. Think about consumerism's driving force of novelty and frequent replacement of goods. For example, when and how does novelty become equated with and valued as progress? How does an annual "need" for new models of products become established and successfully marketed? How does the need for novelty get spread to more different kinds of consumer, commercial, and industrial goods?

Issue #3. Advertising and communication. Questions here involve mass-communication media. How are these media used to maintain and spread such values as the "novelty orientation," which appear to be necessary for present-day consumerism to function?

Issue #4. Explaining apparent alternatives/reactions to consumerism. Even within a consumer society, there are alternatives to rampant consumerism. How do people develop and practice resistance strategies against consumerism? How do people use artifacts to create meanings and identities? How are alternative lifestyles maintained? It is also worth asking how such resistance might be co-opted by the larger society. Specifically, Majewski and Schiffer (2001:33) ask, "How and why do handcrafted products of traditional societies become integrated into the consumption processes of industrial consumer societies?"

Issue #5. Commercialization process of consumer services and societal practices. Among many questions here are those about how religious items and practices and personal services (such as grooming and medical care) become consumerized.

Issue #6. Ideological expressions of consumerist societies. Ideological expressions provide a particularly rich, if somewhat ambiguous, source of questions for material culture studies. I like the way that Majewski and Schiffer state these questions:

> When and how did the ideology of science and technology as founts of wondrous new products become entrenched? How is this ideology related to the artifacts purchased by middle- and working-class people over the last century? How is the erection of monumental architecture in cities since 1850 related to changes in the relative wealth and social power of churches, polities, various kinds of corporations, and sports franchises? (2001:33)

Archaeologists believe that archaeology contributes an important methodology that can address such questions. In thinking about the material culture that we own, or want to own, it is worth some pondering about these issues and questions as they relate to our lives and choices.

SECTION FOUR

Historical Archaeology as Public Scholarship

CHAPTER 24

Introduction to Public Archaeology

Is it possible that the most imperative need today is to acknowledge that the world is not becoming uniform, that national, religious, social, political, cultural and intellectual identities call for a kind of scholarship more respectful of difference, prepared to acknowledge complexity?

—STEPHEN GRAUBARD

It is above all by the imagination that we achieve perception and compassion and hope.

—URSULA K. LeGUIN

Public archaeology has come to mean something far broader than archaeology that's completed to comply with legal and regulatory requirements. It's broader than archaeologists going public to share our knowledge. Public archaeology also includes archaeologists' collaborations with and within communities and our activities in support of civic engagement and civic renewal. At least some segments of the archaeology profession are defining and meeting a growing sense of social responsibility beyond professional self-interest. A socially useful heritage can stimulate and empower local community members, visitors, and scholars to make historically informed judgments about heritage and the ways that we use it in the present. Such work requires imagination and appreciation for the ways that archaeology might connect the past with the difficult and volatile present.

At the beginning of this chapter I quote Stephen Graubard's thought from his recent overview of public scholarship. As the editor of *Daedalus*, the journal of the American Academy of Arts and Sciences, for nearly 40 years, Graubard has a long-term perspective on the important role of the social sciences. He calls for global public scholarship of broad scope. Such scholarship can benefit from the contributions and insights of historical archaeology.

In the following chapters I touch upon several aspects of public historical archaeology. The protection of areas such as parks or other preserves affects relatively small amounts of land, although in many countries federal and other laws seek some balance between destruction and preservation beyond such protected areas. The designation of places on official lists usually implies some measure of protection, although in the United States it is often less protection than its formality implies. Because archaeological resources embody a truly diverse heritage, they are ripe for interpretation and education. Skillful practitioners can provide opportunities to connect past and present in meaningful, relevant ways that can help people cope with change and diversity and support civic renewal and restorative justice. I touch upon the painful past and the culture wars, which often revolve around seemingly opposed opinions about the purpose of history. I end the section with a chapter on the possibilities of transformative learning. I believe there is real opportunity to learn from the past, to embrace the promise of *sankofa*, if we are intentional about the process.

CHAPTER 25

Public Memory and Public Places

Things ain't what they used to be and probably never was.

—WILL ROGERS

The purposes and goals of historical archaeology are often interrelated; preservation, supplementing or challenging history, and reconstructing lifeways are all connected with each other and intertwined with the meanings of the past in today's society. Analyzing material evidence with the purpose of simply finding out "what happened" or discovering something as supposedly straightforward as how people fed themselves can end up challenging taken-for-granted ideas about the past.

The history we learn and know does not depend solely upon the textbooks we struggle through in school, cramming dates and facts for a history test. The history we "know"—and especially the history we know is important—is often absorbed from our surroundings and the places we visit. Writing about the U.S. National Park System, historian Rolf Diamant (2000:41) observes, "The national parks have become, in effect, a living part of our democracy contributing in many ways to the stability and continuity of civil society." The choices made about creating, maintaining (or not), and using parks indicate much about a government's priorities and assumptions. Parks and other forms of commemoration make important contributions to public memory, whether they are government-sponsored sites or privately funded places such as Greenfield Village in Michigan or Colonial Williamsburg in Virginia.

What places are important enough to be preserved in local, state, and national parks? What is considered worth a statue, a plaque, or an inscription? What places appear in our registers of historic places? What are the places we recognize in our local communities? We are surrounded by layers upon layers of varying and sometimes conflicting material expressions about history.

These places and objects on the landscape are an important part of our public memory because such commemoration is the explicit creation of heritage memorialized in the built environment. Paul Shackel (2003:11) writes, "Public memory is more a reflection of present political and social relations than a true reconstruction of the past. As present conditions change socially, politically, and ideologically, the collective memory of the past will also change." Will Rogers' quote reminds us that we cannot really get there from here, that our recall of the past is quite imperfect.

What is important enough to study, to commemorate, to interpret? Answers will differ widely. The ways archaeologists prioritize archaeological research and elevate certain time periods or resources into the category of "things worth studying" are clearly related to judgments about what is interesting enough or important enough to preserve or interpret to the public.

Acts of commemoration include official designations on lists of historic places, creating protected lands like national parks, building monuments or memorials, and offering interpretation in the public sphere, some of which we touched on in chapter 3. Acts of commemoration in the public sphere and acts of scholarly legitimization in the academic sphere are connected and sometimes mirror each other. Each intersects with the profit-driven heritage tourism destinations. Each must somehow come to terms with the wider social, political, and economic context in which it is performed.

What are the politics of commemoration that impinge on choices about presentation of histories and archaeologies? Where does archaeology fit within nation-building and nationalism? How do we balance our understanding that present perceptions of the past cannot be completely accurate with the desire to remember and learn from a representative, inclusive, and true history? I want to explore some of the implications of heritage areas as places of public historical commemoration and then turn to Elmina Castle and Dungeons in Ghana, where Ghanaians and African Americans are in conflict over preservation and presentation.

Governments at all levels still create parks. However, such public land ownership is no longer as prominent a method of protecting naturally or culturally significant areas. Globally, there has been a revolution in thinking about protected areas over the last 40 years, breaking away from a top-down, government-knows-best model. Currently there are more actors in the protection of lands and the scale is much bigger. There has been a shift from creating new bounded areas of federal ownership to large, living landscapes with multiple owners and complex partnerships based on shared management and multiple objectives.

At least in the U.S., most heritage areas have not come about through governmental advocacy, but are the result of grassroots efforts. The people involved have demanded governmental recognition. Laws that officially recognize a place as a heritage area carry with them implications of governmental technical assistance and some economic assistance in the form of loans, grants, tax credits, cost sharing, and tourism marketing. There are important issues in these heritage areas concerning identity, power, and control over the past, present, and future. The kinds of partnership and cooperation needed for a heritage area take a great deal of sustained effort. Any such arrangement must cope with ongoing tension among academics, historically minded locals, business-minded locals, tourism developers, and governmental agencies, and address common heritage issues such as meaning, control, participation, funding, and economic development.

In many cases, the underlying motive for preservation is less about tourism or outsiders than about identifying and preserving aspects of heritage that residents consider essential to their identity and the character of the region. Brenda Barrett is the director of the heritage areas program for the U.S. National Park Service. She and her coauthor Augie Carlino explain:

> Most heritage area initiatives arise in communities that are under stress: losing their traditional economic base, whether it is industry or farming; facing a loss of population, particularly young people; or growing rapidly with an influx of people who do not know the old stories or the history of the region. It is no surprise that communities across the nation are looking at this new kind of partnership to preserve what they care about as they face an uncertain future. It is no surprise that heritage areas appeal to regions that are trying to preserve some element of the authentic past in a culture that is moving toward uniformity and sameness. (2003:52)

The creation and development of heritage areas raise any number of critical issues related to the ways that we understand, study, and commemorate the past. These issues are directly relevant to the ways in which historical archaeologists and other heritage professionals do their work in a public context. These issues also intersect with the ways that such places figure in civic renewal and in the creation of social capital, issues I'll take up in chapter 29.

How do the heritage and the area get defined and by whom? This question highlights some fairly obvious goals. One is to define the participants. Another is to seek a fuller understanding of what our heritage is, or perhaps more accurately (if less elegantly) what our heritages are. Another is to seek what those heritages mean.

The method for learning these things, borrowed from anthropology and other social sciences, is to ask and listen. It is important to initiate and maintain a dialogue that is as socially inclusive as possible. Heritage themes get identified from outside as well as inside a community. There are insiders and outsiders of many kinds, including academics, media, and governments, as well as residents and visitors.

At a basic level, social inclusion means seeking out the nonrepresented, that is, identifying who is not at the table and inviting them. It often falls to the heritage professionals to identify the interested public and to perform outreach that gets more of the public interested and willing to participate. Heritage area residents face the challenge of clearly expressing what heritage is, as do visitors, whatever their motivation for visiting. Social inclusion means expanding interpretive space and opportunities for cultural transmission and involvement.

This raises a second category of heritage issues. That is, what are the politics and economics of identifying and maintaining such heritage? Local politics cannot be separated from decisions about who is invited to participate in planning dialogues. The ideal goal, of course, is to have full participation from within communities. Because the public is integral to the process, it is useful for community members to learn skills of self-reflection and apply them to heritage dialogues.

These points about heritage lead me to a case example that raises questions about ownership and rights. The Portuguese built Elmina Castle on the west coast of Ghana in 1482. As one of the staging areas for the transatlantic slave trade, this massive structure, which overlooks an archaeological site and dominates the landscape, evokes strong feelings. It also has evoked hope for Ghana's developing tourism industry.

Anthropologist Edward Bruner analyzes the tensions surrounding this tourism. African American tourists and the local Ghanaian people have very different experiences, historical backgrounds, and expectations for these slave castles. Ghanaians have high hopes for the profitability of tourism and want to attract paying visitors. Because of the brutal way that their ancestors were captured, warehoused, and shipped, many African Americans see the dungeons as sacred ground. In general they don't want the castles to be painted or cleaned up and made beautiful, but rather to convey their past horror.

The Ghanaians are not as concerned with the history of slavery, although their ancestors participated in the transatlantic trade by providing captives to Europeans. They focus on the longer history of the place. The Dutch captured Elmina from the Portuguese in 1637 and converted the Catholic Church inside the castle into a slave auction market. The British gained control of West Africa in 1872. Ghana achieved independence in 1957 and the castle served miscellaneous purposes including school and office space before being turned into a tourism destination. The Ghanaian museum professionals and their partners consider the interests of a wide range of tourists. The Dutch tourists tend to be interested in the Dutch period and the Dutch cemetery. The British want to know about colonial rule on the Gold Coast. The Ashanti want to see the room where their King Prempeh I was imprisoned in 1896 after the British defeat of their kingdom. The king is important to all Ghanaians because he represents resistance to colonialism.

As Bruner (1996:293) summarizes, "Ghanaians want the castles restored, with good lighting and heating, so they will be attractive to tourists; African Americans want the castles to be as they see them—a cemetery for the slaves who died in the dungeons' inhuman conditions while waiting for the ships to transport them to the Americas."

As conflicts over the site escalated, Ghana's National Commission of Culture held a conference in 1994 to decide on guidelines for the highly contested conservation. In addition to closing the restaurant at Cape Coast Castle and deciding that such facilities should be allowed only outside, the commission agreed to change the names of both Elmina and Cape Coast from "Castle" to "Castle and Dungeons."

The naming is significant, but the question remains: which version or versions of history should be told? Some diasporic Africans have the sense that these castles "belong" to them. Indeed, UNESCO makes it clear on their website (http://whc.unesco.org/) on World Heritage Sites—and the forts and castles of Ghana are recognized as such—that these sites "belong to all the peoples of the world, irrespective of the territory on which they are located." What does that mean for the way such places are conserved and marketed? What does it mean for the local community in Elmina and the nation of Ghana?

In heritage places of all kinds we can find unique difficulties embedded in both the local and the global. The face of "heritage" is potentially isolating as a set of memories into which it is possible for people to withdraw and exclude others or make invisible some parts of the past. Certain stories can be deemed acceptable while others are not. This is one place where the outsider—the heritage professional—may play an invaluable role as facilitator to assist in identifying and suspending power differentials within a dialogue so that dialogue includes all of the stories and allows for the kinds of education, civic renewal, and transformation we'll explore in the following chapters.

CHAPTER 26

Education and Outreach

There is the challenge! To put your visitor in possession of at least one disturbing idea that may grow into a fruitful interest.

—FREEMAN TILDEN

Communication with and for the public is a booming enterprise among archaeologists, who see outreach and public involvement as more important than ever before. As you may remember from our discussion of ethics in chapter 13, archaeologists perceive public support as being tied to the very survival of the archaeological resource base.

Every sector of the archaeological profession considers public education and outreach to be important. Private contract firms of all sizes incorporate elements of public outreach into at least some projects. Public outreach is integral to the work of many private foundations. Governments at every level are rightly concerned with the public benefit of the work they require or sponsor. Therefore, they often want educational or interpretive products such as lesson plans, pamphlets, and exhibits in addition to research reports and databases. Some academic institutions are engaged in outreach efforts connected to civic engagement and service learning. Colleges and universities are also responding to the demands of the workplace for which their students are destined. They are incorporating education and interpretation into the curriculum. An increasing number of schools are including archaeology in elementary and high school education as well.

Why is history—from oral, documentary, and material sources—necessary for us as educated citizens? The methodological and theoretical tools needed to make interpretations equips us to think critically and to make judgments about the information with which we are bombarded every day. Because stories about the past are used for many purposes—both noble and nefarious—

each of us must be in a position to judge those stories for ourselves. Learning the methods, logic, important questions, and some of the results of scholarly inquiry helps us all to sort the truth from lies and misrepresentations.

The U.S. National Standards for History set out the significance of history for the educated citizen. One of the primary qualities history conveys is competence in a multicultural world, a skill useful across the globe. The National Center for History in the Schools explains:

> Today's students, more than ever before, need also a comprehensive understanding of the history of the world, and of the peoples of many different cultures and civilizations who have developed ideas, institutions, and ways of life different from the students' own. From a balanced and inclusive world history students may gain an appreciation both of the world's many cultures and of their shared humanity and common problems.... Especially important, an understanding of the history of the world's many cultures can contribute to fostering the kind of mutual patience, respect, and civic courage required in our increasingly pluralistic society and our increasingly interdependent world. (1996:1)

If educators are intentional about it, archaeology can teach some of the essential skills for coping with an increasingly complex world. Educator Fay Metcalf has worked to bring archaeology into the classroom because she sees it as a way to help challenge and dismantle many of the myths and lies believed by so many children and adults. The process by which archaeologists create knowledge is of particular interest to her:

> Going "beyond the facts" to see contradictions and paradoxes and still coming up with generalizations is what archaeologists do every day. Archaeologists are the synthesizers, putting things together, combining and recombining. Consequently, archaeologists are great role models for students who will have to puzzle out how to make decisions in the twenty-first century. (Metcalf 2002:175)

Many of the efforts to get archaeology into the classroom aim to teach children not only logic and critical thinking skills, but also about other cultures and other times and thereby to understand current diversity better. "Visiting" other times and other cultures through archaeology shows students that some parts of others' experiences are similar to their own, while other parts are very different. Such learning can open one's eyes to diversity in the present.

Of course, archaeological education and outreach are not limited to schools. In archaeological parlance, interpretation usually refers to an analytical process of drawing results or conclusions out of the data. In the world of public outreach and site presentation, the National Association for Interpretation defines interpretation as a "communication process that forges emotional and intellectual connections between the interests of the audience and the inherent meanings in the resource."

Because of the deeply embedded interdisciplinary nature of our work, archaeologists tend to be inveterate borrowers from other disciplines. We'll experiment with just about anything that looks promising. We have found the various arts of interpretation attractive as we've come to understand public outreach as increasingly important. Archaeologists are looking for proven ways to engage the general public in places outside of the classroom because visitors often struggle to understand context and relevance of an exhibit or historic place. It is very difficult to understand how a particular historical event or place fits into the bigger picture. If the significance is unclear, then how can history be relevant to contemporary life?

Interpreters aim to provide relevance through universal concepts. One of the current tenets of interpretation involves the linking of tangible resources (such as a teacup, an awl handle, or a landscape) to intangible resources (such as beauty, danger, loss, life, death) in order to suggest or reveal meanings. Interpreters define universal concepts as intangible resources that almost everyone can relate to and therefore provide the greatest degree of relevance and meaning to the greatest number of people. Often this sort of linking acts as an effective hook to pull in an audience. It is a direct legacy of writer Freeman Tilden, whose work has exerted phenomenal influence on the goals and methods of interpretation over the last half century.

Janet Spector's work offers archaeologists an example of telling an effective story through linking a specific artifact to a larger experience. In *What This Awl Means: Feminist Archaeology at a Wahpeton Dakota Village*, Spector tells interconnected stories. She tells her personal story of bringing feminist insights to historical archaeology. She struggled with identifying gender in material remains by tying together artifacts, gender-specific tasks, and documentary sources. Dissatisfied with both the process and the result, she instead came to focus on a single artifact as an evocative entry into Dakota experience. Spector's primary narrative is that of the Eastern Dakota (Sioux) people in the early to mid-1800s at the village site of Little Rapids in Minnesota. A decorated bone awl handle lost by a Dakota woman inspired her to write a fictional narrative centered on a young girl who uses the awl to do quill work and bead moccasins. This tangible artifact of the bone awl handle connects us with the woman and her tribe's history through the intangible and universal experience of loss and its many reverberations. Spector intertwines these stories with the archaeological information, albeit in a nontraditional way.

We'll explore the concept of the painful past in the next chapter, but consider how the acknowledgment of universal experiences of pain, struggle, and sorrow serve the positive purpose of heightening empathy but may not offer any insight into the lessons that such history could offer. In balancing content and presentation, I find it helpful to think about the distinction between a story and a plot. A story is a series of events. The audience for a story asks, "And then? And then?" as a story demands only curiosity. On the other hand, a plot is based on causality and demands intelligence and memory, as the audience asks, "Why?" It is worth considering that the story that only seeks to tug on universal emotions doesn't need a "why" or a historically based explanation of conflict or controversy.

Interpreting the "why" demands more scholarly and artistic responsibility. Plot, therefore, may be necessary if many of the insights archaeologists gain are to be part of our storytelling. Stories may be reconceptualized as plot so that visitors' intellects are as explicitly engaged as their emotions. It demands the sort of imagination that author Ursula LeGuin refers to in the quote I used for the introductory thoughts to this section. (It is telling that LeGuin, daughter of the very influential anthropologist Alfred Kroeber, turned to fiction to relay her understandings of the human condition.) The skill to suggest cause and effect also requires an ability to suggest that explanations might be incomplete or under constant reexamination and revision, which is always the case with archaeological results.

CHAPTER 27

What About the Painful Past?

History, despite its wrenching pain, cannot be unlived, but if faced with courage, need not be lived again.

—MAYA ANGELOU

One of the most remarkable developments of the last quarter of the 20th century was the creation of truth commissions in many countries. These commissions have served as a tool for conflict resolution and for the peaceful reconciliation of victims and state-sponsored victimizers. They seek a peaceful way forward out of a past characterized by violence and injustice by giving both victims (or their survivors) and perpetrators an official forum to testify about human rights abuses. Such commissions make abuses public and create recommendations for preventing future abuses. Truth commissions have done important work all over the world. In South Africa, the Commission of Truth and Reconciliation, chaired by Anglican Archbishop Desmond Tutu, was set up in 1995 to investigate Apartheid-era (1960–1994) human rights violations.

Archbishop Tutu has described the concept of restorative justice in the truth and reconciliation process. He contrasts it with retributive justice, which is punitive and aimed at making sure that the offender is punished:

> *Ubuntu* is the essence of being human. We say a person is a person through other persons. We are made for togetherness, to live in a delicate network of interdependence.... For *ubuntu* the *summum bonum*, the greatest good is communal harmony. Anger, hatred, resentment all are corrosive of this good. If one person is dehumanised then inexorably we are all diminished and dehumanised in our turn.... [T]he Truth and Reconciliation Commission was based on the premise that people retained the capacity to change, that enemies could become friends.

Ubuntu and so restorative justice gives up on no-one. No-one is a totally hopeless and irredeemable case.... We can say that the principles of *ubuntu* have helped in our case in South Africa to avert a catastrophe of monumental proportions in substituting forgiveness for revenge and reconciliation for retribution. (2004)

The key for potential success of public truth-telling is for the testimony to reveal information that was otherwise denied, hidden, or distorted. How can we connect this important insight to our historical studies? Incomplete and exclusionary histories serve to conceal the truth about the past—truth that is needed if we are indeed to learn from the experiences of our predecessors and to attempt to heal long-standing wounds.

Historian Eric Foner (2002:11) notes that social history has made some progress in expanding our understanding and that because of it "we today have a far more complete and nuanced portrait of the American past, in all its diversity and contentiousness." Historical archaeology is part of that social history effort and has been inspired by it. The uses of historical archaeology in a process of coping with the legacies of difficult histories may be limited, but they are powerful in particular situations. The importance of truthful history cannot be overestimated. Such truthfulness at best can strive toward an approximation and must acknowledge the ambiguities and tensions that abide in histories that seek to include everyone's pasts and the meanings of those pasts. Such a multivocal history may not always sound harmonious, but it is realistic and it acknowledges the worthiness of all people's lives.

Truth commissions are responses to the very recent past, but some of the concepts behind them can be adapted by historical archaeologists interested in using investigations of the deeper past as one tool for social reconciliation. Archaeology can contribute to truth-telling by revealing or highlighting hidden or denied parts of the past. Such revelation may come about through creating a more inclusive history and one that can be seen in different ways. Archaeologists are famous for searching for origins in the quest for "firsts" and do so because origin stories have powerful mythological resonance in many cultures. Part of the questioning that guides research is a search for beginnings and root causes. In searching for the origins of persistent and pervasive wrongs, particularly pernicious culturally embedded ones like racism, we are likely to find the quarry elusive. Although we are not likely to uncover the ultimate genealogy of oppression, there are some historical, cultural shifts that are worth analyzing and reanalyzing, if only to understand that history is contingent rather than inevitable or predetermined. Learning that the way that the past played out was neither inevitable nor preordained helps to open more possibilities for the future.

One of the most publicized sites in historical archaeology in the United States is the African Burial Ground in lower Manhattan, a block north of New York City Hall. Like many sites, this cemetery was discovered during a routine investigation done to comply with the National Historic Preservation Act. The U.S. General Services Administration (a federal agency that manages government property) planned new construction at Foley Square near Broadway and contracted for the mandated work. Although a "Negroes Burial Ground" was indicated on 18th-century maps, many archaeologists and historians assumed that the cemetery had been obliterated by subsequent construction in the densely built city. That assumption proved to be quite wrong. Excavation began to uncover human skeletal remains buried under 16 to 28 feet of fill. From 1991 to 1992 excavators disinterred over 400 burials in a small portion of what was once a five- to six-acre burial ground. I can only understate the response: a massive public outcry ensued. The descendant community got involved and has remained involved in every aspect of the project, from research design to education, to reinterment and memorialization.

The African Burial Ground was established by 1712 at the latest and its official use ended in 1794. During this time the city was under English and then American rule. Prior to New York, of course, was New Amsterdam, founded in 1624 by the Dutch West India Company at the lower end of Manhattan Island. Almost immediately after settling, the Dutch had begun to import African captives. England conquered the colony in 1664 and the population of enslaved Africans in the city continued to grow. Gradual emancipation did not begin in New York State until 1799 and it was largely effective by 1827.

Some documentary evidence hints at whites' attempts to control blacks by creating rules about funerals and funeral customs and restricting the numbers of people allowed to attend. In 1722, for example, the Common Council legally banned night funerals. As for the archaeological evidence, the skeletal remains themselves demonstrate with appalling clarity other types of control, violence, and restrictions.

The researchers used three organizing themes for their study: origins and arrivals of Africans in colonial New York, life and death in New York, and the transformations involved in adapting to the New World. Additionally, the project was centered on the meaning of the ancestors to the descendant

FIGURE 11. Memorial stone at the African Burial Ground, New York City, donated by the country of Nigeria and dedicated September 22, 2004. (*Photo by author*)

community. As biological anthropologist and project director Michael Blakey (2004:25) describes: "The study's focus was on revealing the diasporic experiences of the enslaved New York Africans, the history and identity of their descendants, and their descendants' empowerment in telling their own story and memorializing their own ancestors."

During the first part of the 18th century, imports of captive Africans came into New York from the West Indies. After the 1740s, importation tended to be directly from Africa, as it had been during the 17th century. Most individuals would have come from West and West Central Africa. A shift in labor needs affected the slave trade. Most slaveholdings were small, with one to three laborers who worked as farm laborers, domestics, dockworkers, construction workers, or craftsmen. The 18th century saw an increased desire for domestic servants. Because girls were considered ready for domestic work at a very young age, the importation of girls from Africa greatly affected the African population in the city and, ultimately, in the burial ground.

The analysis of both skeletal remains and the artifacts provides the evidence for some details about national origin, health, work, and death. There are several distinctive burials. The man who was buried in the coffin decorated with the heart-shaped symbol made of tacks, evocative of the *sankofa* symbol, appears to have been born in Africa, as his teeth had been filed according to

African custom into hourglass shapes. Another native-born African also had filed teeth and wore strings of glass beads and cowrie shells around her waist.

Judging by all available evidence, the enslaved Africans and African Americans were a population very highly stressed by malnutrition, infection, poor medical care, lead pollution, overwork, and injury. The skeletons of both women and men exhibit results of arduous work. Characteristics of physical stress show load bearing near the upper spine in women and the lower spine in men. Both exhibit degenerative joint disease and muscle hypertrophy, that is, enlarged muscle attachments in their limbs. The physical effects of enslavement were as severe in New York as anywhere.

Although importation continued and enslaved women bore children, analysis of the remains in the burial ground indicate that there was little or no growth in the 18th-century African population. The researchers investigate the reasons for this abnormal pattern and conclude that the economic strategy on the part of the slave owners and slave traders was intentional:

> Economic strategy was one of "unlimited good," since enslaved captives could be replaced continuously. European enslavers had no incentive for encouraging fertility or intensive care giving of infants, who demanded high investment but could do little work. Although the abusive practices of the British Caribbean colonies, where infants might be taken from their mothers immediately so that loss of labor would be minimized, are not documented for New York, this city's slaveholders showed no desire to possess young Africans or to "breed" their captives. They only needed them to keep the market's products and profits flowing. (Blakey et al. 2004a:539)

Participants in the African Burial Ground project succeeded in creating a collaborative effort among the various voices of the descendant and local community, religious leaders, politicians, community activists, many different scholars, and several governmental agencies. The project team did not restrict the definition of the descendant community to African Americans in New York or even the United States. They also reached out to Africans. When the skeletal remains were reburied, they were placed in new coffins carved in Ghana. Nigeria provided the stone laid during reinterment ceremonies in 2004.

The researchers took great care to consider the meaning of the ancestors to the descendant community. Cheryl LaRoche and Michael Blakey summarize the public engagement of the project:

As the situation in New York evolved, the African Burial Ground became apparent as a practical and dramatic case for the development of the theory and practice of inclusion and engagement. In the case of the African Burial Ground,
engagement was also powerfully informed by the long tradition of African-
American vindicationist critique. (1997:99)

The term "vindicationist" comes from a long tradition of African American
scholarship that counters racism and racial denigration with a combination of
academic work and social activism.

The archaeology of the African Burial Ground project provides an opportunity to learn about 18th-century slavery in the North, a part of history less
familiar to most Americans than southern plantation slavery. In that way, the
project reveals more of the truth of the painful past. However, in this case the
archaeology provides more than evidence; it provides a gateway to *sankofa*.
LaRoche and Blakey (1997:100) explain, "Archaeology is not an end in itself.
For many African Americans, it is a conduit, an avenue leading to spiritual
rebirth and renewal of our history."

CHAPTER 28

History and the Culture Wars

History, real solemn history, I cannot be interested in. I read it a little as a duty, but it tells me nothing that does not either vex or weary me. The quarrels of popes and kings, with wars or pestilences, in every page; the men all so good for nothing, and hardly any women at all—it is very tiresome.
—JANE AUSTEN, NORTHANGER ABBEY

In a 1935 presentation to the American Planning and Civic Association, Verne E. Chatelain, the first Chief Historian of the National Park Service, promoted a celebratory view of history. He viewed places commemorated by national parks as areas where "stirring" significant events occurred. Chatelain highlighted not only their

> importance in themselves but their integral relationship to the whole history of American development. In other words, the task is to breathe the breath of life into American history for those to whom it has been a dull recital of meaningless facts—to recreate for the average citizen something of the color, the pageantry, and the dignity of our national past. (Mackintosh 1986)

Dwight Pitcaithley, the National Park Service Chief Historian from 1995 to 2005, also writes with citizenship in mind, but with a broader and more complex perception of the relationship between citizenship and history. He writes:

> Our goal is to offer a window into the historical richness of the National Park System and the opportunity it presents for understanding who we are, where we have been and how we as a society might approach the future. This collection of special places also allows us to examine our past—the contested along with the

comfortable, the complex along with the simple, the controversial along with the inspirational. (Diamant 2000:40–41)

These two views of history as celebratory and challenging are often echoed in current, often vociferous debates about the content and meaning of national history and culture. They are not genuinely mutually exclusive, although you wouldn't get that sense from the self-righteous tone that permeates the divisive debate. Instead, the celebratory and challenging views of history usefully challenge each other as we consider the benefits of heritage, knowledge of the past, and inquiries into the human condition. How do we, here and now, fit into the expansive course of history? This is a question for each of us as we ponder our relationships with the land and our fellow inhabitants, both contemporary and historical. How might we allow ourselves to be inspired by others' struggles and persistence, rather than wishing for, and even creating, a sanitized and falsely harmonious past?

Museums and historic places tend to be on the front lines in the battles that are fought in the history wars and the culture wars. Such battles come to the public forefront in cases of well-publicized exhibits like that of the *Enola Gay* at the Smithsonian's Air and Space Museum. The museum planned a new exhibit to mark the 50th anniversary of the atomic bombing of Hiroshima on August 6, 1945. The *Enola Gay* was the airplane used to drop the bomb and the original exhibit plan was to include not only the reasons behind using the bomb to end the war but also discussion of the effects of the bomb: the nightmare for the victims and the global aftermath of the terror of nuclear war. The exhibit plan sparked an intense controversy. On one side were those who accused the Smithsonian of revising history to denigrate American heroes by calling into question decisions made during wartime. On the other side were those who called for telling the story of the *Enola Gay* in a much broader context and from today's vantage point, including the unforeseen consequences of the bombing. What might we learn from the exhibit plan and the reactions to it? What do we need to learn from the past? And what might we learn from the bitterly polarized debate about the fears and hopes that drive each side?

Mark Bograd and Theresa Singleton take a critical look at the representation of slavery at a few historic houses and living history museums. They summarize their findings:

The characterization of slavery at Mount Vernon and Monticello is best characterized as mostly benign and, occasionally, willfully neglectful. One detects an underlying concern: that to interpret slavery tarnishes the memory of the heroes Washington and Jefferson.... We have to ask ourselves whether their significant accomplishments are diminished by their roles as slave owners. (1997:203)

At both of these presidential houses, as well as at Jefferson's Poplar Forest retreat, James Madison's Montpelier, Andrew Jackson's Hermitage, and at Colonial Williamsburg, archaeology has been an important catalyst and source of information for including slavery in public interpretations.

Historical archaeology in the United States is rarely a magnet for highly emotional and public contests about the meaning of the past, but that is not true in some other countries. Several African countries have used archaeology to reclaim the past denied them during colonization. To deny that Africans were capable of civilization, colonial Rhodesia tried to give the astonishing site of Great Zimbabwe a foreign, non-African identity. Reclaiming the past, in this case, also meant renaming the country. As Innocent Pikirayi (2006:246) points out, "Zimbabwe, for instance, is the only country in the world named after an archaeological site."

Likewise, in Latin America, the restoration of civilian rule in several countries, particularly in Brazil, has opened the door to a booming historical archaeology. You don't have to be a particularly avid follower of events in the Middle East to appreciate the powerful meaning of the archaeological and historical past for Jewish, Islamic, and Christian factions, or of events in India to understand the passion surrounding Hindu and Islamic monuments and sites. Excavations and archaeological interpretations are often extremely contentious. Wherever it is done, forensic archaeology that identifies victims of state terror and genocidal campaigns is highly emotionally charged. In the United States, slavery and its aftermath are highly charged issues. Historical archaeology projects that focus on such issues can draw intense interest. At the African Burial Ground in New York City, as mentioned in previous chapters, the archaeological, historical, and skeletal biology research has been under public scrutiny since its inception in the early 1990s. However, government actions and the politics of scholarship, rather than archaeology per se, have been lightning rods for public outrage over this excavation.

It seems likely to me that historical archaeology will find itself at the center of widely publicized controversies. The cultural meanings of material culture and historic places, after all, spark many of these debates, and historical archaeology will be involved in public debates over the past and what it means to us in the present. In the 1930s historical archaeology joined the social history of the time in creating and supporting national patriotism. Certainly historical archaeology has never abandoned that role and still contributes to heritage and national myth. But it also has an important role to play in providing different ways to look at the past.

Much of the rhetoric of the "culture wars" centers on history and gains its strength through the deep and widespread belief that a shared history and shared knowledge of that history are necessary for national unity and identity. Of course, it is not at all self-evident what either a shared history or identity may entail. Sometimes those who perceive a need for shared history seek to mythologize the past and create perfect heroes out of simple human beings. Mythologizing and dehumanizing such heroes stands in the way of honest history. It is important to ask why we may feel the need to consider people who have preceded us as anything other than human beings, deeply flawed as all human beings are and ever have been.

Should a history of shared American experience rest on an edited view of the past? Is the American identity so weak that a true and inclusive history shatters it? Can we instead consider a lesson from South Africa's Truth and Reconciliation Commission's final report, as it explains the need to confront the painful past:

> There were others who urged that the past should be forgotten—glibly declaring that we should "let bygones by bygones." This option was rejected because such amnesia would have resulted in further victimisation of victims by denying their awful experiences....The other reason amnesia simply will not do is that the past refuses to lie down quietly. It has an uncanny habit of returning to haunt one. "Those who forget the past are doomed to repeat it" are the words emblazoned at the entrance to the museum in the former concentration camp of Dachau. They are words we would do well to keep ever in mind. However painful the experience, the wounds of the past must not be allowed to fester. They must be opened. They must be cleansed. And balm just be poured on them so they can heal. This is not to be obsessed with the past. It is to take care that the past is properly dealt with for the sake of the future.

History must be inclusive. As Jane Austen's character Catherine Morland, quoted at the beginning of this chapter, reminds us, individuals may not see any relevance for themselves in a history that leaves them out. What does it mean for you if your own identity is not taught or included in your country's history and therefore ignored as part of an essential national identity? What does it mean for your sense of entitlement if only your history and identity are acknowledged? The best tradition of the humanities is that we all share the common ground of human identity and can learn and be enriched by others' experiences.

Authenticity requires appreciating the great diversity and complexity of the past. If we are fortunate, such appreciation translates into a better understanding and celebration of diversity today. Some insist on editing our understanding of the past, often focusing nearly exclusively on what is judged good or patriotically appropriate. But how can we expect to learn from the past if we don't see it complete with mistakes and disgraces as well as actions we judge as heroic?

CHAPTER 29

Civic Renewal and Restorative Justice

The places that commemorate sad history are not places in which we wallow, or wallow in remorse, but instead places in which we may be moved to a new resolve, to be better citizens.... Explaining history from a variety of angles makes it not only more interesting, but also more true. When it is more true, more people come to feel that they have a part in it. That is where patriotism and loyalty intersect with truth.

—JOHN HOPE FRANKLIN

The goals of the civic renewal movement include community building, the creation of social capital, and active citizen engagement in community and civic life. Archaeology per se is not usually seen as an explicit part of this movement. However, archaeologists have a role to play, particularly as projects increasingly involve the communities in which they occur and the descendants of the people whose lives are the subject of study.

At the same time, archaeology is still firmly situated in the heritage movement, which is certainly tied into citizens' longing for connections and identity. Historian David Lowenthal (1998:78) has written that "History is still mostly written by the winners. But heritage increasingly belongs to the losers." Can heritage be rehabilitated as a source of social and political empowerment?

Social capital may be defined as goodwill, fellowship, and the social interactions that count in the daily lives of people who make up any social unit. Social capital gives rise to connections of trust, reciprocity, shared values, and networks among individuals. There are two basic kinds of social capital. "Bonding social capital" is exclusive and homogenizing. That is, it builds internal cohesion within a group, however that group is defined. "Bridging social capital" is inclusive and acts across social divides. It is important to distinguish between these two forms because strong communities with abundant social capital can coalesce around values that are not targeted toward the greater good. Group solidarity, supported by bonding social capital, is often purchased at the cost of hostility toward outsiders. Alison Wylie is a philosopher of science who studies archaeology extensively. She has hinted at the bonding and bridging functions of the discipline. She writes (1994:10) of the opposite capacities of archaeology to "incorporate and reproduce racist, nationalist, and other agendas, *and* its democratising power, its capacity to counter 'mythologies'... and to support decisive critical reexamination of the assumptions that both inform and are promoted by these agendas." Her analysis suggests that the discipline is never neutral but is profoundly embedded in social politics, an observation that highlights archaeologists' responsibilities to the public.

We already have seen many examples of archaeologists collaborating with communities, including the Monacan tribe in Virginia, African Americans and Africans with the African Burial Ground project in Manhattan, residents of West Oakland, California, with the Cypress Freeway replacement project, and the local and descendant communities involved with many of the other sites mentioned in this book. There are many other examples and, as archaeologists become more committed to civic renewal, there will be more and more. Work with communities ranges widely in degree, from nearly no involvement to full collaboration. Community members may become involved in a project through providing oral history, providing items for exhibits, or contributing ideas, labor, or funds. Communities may be in the driver's seat, for example contracting with archaeologists to run excavations and educational programs. In some cases, archaeologists and communities collaborate fully on every aspect of the project, from research design through the dissemination of the results. Often local communities are very interested in the possible tourism draw of an archaeological project. Just as often, community members find archaeology compelling for what it offers in further defining and maintaining the identity of the community.

Charles Orser has worked on plantation and tenant farms in the southeastern United States, Palmares in Brazil, and 19th-century rural sites in Ireland. He is interested in the tensions between archaeologists and communities, particularly when interpretations clash and communities want to see the past represented in their own terms (as do, of course, the archaeologists). Working in Ireland, he has found that he must consider not only the local community, but also the intense interest of the worldwide Irish diasporic community who consider Ireland and specific counties their ancestral home.

Seemingly simple choices take on great importance for these Irish communities, signaling loyalties and preconceptions; for example, it is highly significant whether one calls the defining event of mid-19th-century Ireland the Great Starvation, the Great Famine, the Great Hunger, the Irish Holocaust, or the Irish Potato Famine. The point is that history—including that made through historical archaeology—matters to the Irish and to those of Irish descent.

Orser is working on sites in Ballykilcline in north County Roscommon, an area with a turbulent past of tensions and violence between landlords and tenants, between British and Irish. Community members are intensely interested in Orser's project. In particular, some of his project's findings about household ceramics have become deeply significant. Two house sites reveal that residents owned and used both Irish-made and English ceramics. The Irish ware is utilitarian earthenware made for kitchen and dairy, including milk pans, storage crocks, and jugs. The English ware is mainly teacups, plates, and saucers of refined decorated earthenware.

Both the community and the archaeologists want to know how these people obtained their ceramics. Orser offers three possibilities for the more expensive English ceramics in particular: purchase, theft, or gifts. He tends to favor the first option, but the questions raised by the community appropriately complicate the analysis. Some residents think that theft is more likely, both because of abject poverty and their understanding that theft from the English would have been seen as honorable and overtly defiant. Others question the archaeologists' reliance on English documents and the interpretations that such documents suggest, concerned that past racist attitudes toward the Irish may be perpetuated in the present. Orser (2004:187) willingly complicates his research with further questions, remarking that "without interaction with both members of the diasporic community and residents to its homeland, such questions would have been much more difficult to frame, let alone to address."

In many cases of working with communities, archaeologists find themselves working with museums as well. Museums have been redefining their social roles over the last few decades and many are deeply involved in civic engagement and renewal. In asking questions about what museums can offer, museum scholar Stephen Weil emphasizes the importance of service to society. He emphasizes that the goal of a museum is to improve people's lives. He and others write about the museum's need to confront social, political, cultural, and ethical issues and call for museums to take on central community roles as places to explore social issues. One of the important things that museums can do is to stimulate and empower visitors and community members so that they can make "better informed judgment about their own past and more insightful choices about their future" (Weil 1990:55).

In a very influential article, Ed Chappell, the director of architectural research at Colonial Williamsburg, writes:

> At their worst, they [historical museums] make evil in the past seem romantic and inequality in the present seem inevitable. At their best, museums [and historic sites] help people to understand the rifts that separate us from one another. The time has come to stop adjusting the furniture and begin reforming our essential presentations of the past. (1989:265)

The new museology calls for civic engagement, a commitment far beyond that of public education. Archaeologists, along with their colleagues in museums of all kinds, often are well situated to participate.

The International Coalition of Historic Site Museums of Conscience was founded in 1999 by individuals committed to the idea that historic sites have an obligation to assist the public in drawing connections between history and its contemporary implications. Part of the coalition's declaration reads:

> The goal is to transform historic site museums from places of passive learning to places of active citizen engagement. We seek to use the history of what happened at our sites—whether it was genocide, a violation of civil rights, or a triumph of democracy—as the foundation for dialogue about how and where these issues are alive today, and about what can be done to address them.

Members of this international coalition use various methods of civic engagement, including focus groups, structured dialogue in a format they call "dialogues for democracy," community projects, and often specific projects focused on youth or teachers and education. Community projects may not always be geographically focused because interested communities can be quite far-flung, including descendant, national, and academic communities.

The Lower East Side Tenement Museum in New York City is one of the founders of the coalition. This museum owns a tenement building occupied in the 19th century by immigrants and interprets the challenges and struggles of historical immigrants, linking them directly to the lives of today's immigrants. Although there are many differences—countries of origin, religion, occupations—and it is a different world, many of the challenges facing immigrants of the past and present are similar. The museum offers tours and opportunities for active engagement so that people can draw useful lessons, models, and examples for coping with these challenges. Their programs offer examples of creating opportunities for bridging social capital. Rather than drawing dividing lines between the struggles of "us" and "them," such work seeks to unite people through shared struggle and shared goals of creating viable and meaningful lives.

Archaeologists are now approaching difficult pasts and explicitly connecting the past with the difficult present. It will be helpful if we can become comfortable with ambiguity, discontinuity, discomfort, and unease. As we work with communities, we can help each other to enrich the present and the future.

CHAPTER 30

Transformative Learning and Archaeology

All right then, I'll go to hell.
—MARK TWAIN, *THE ADVENTURES OF HUCKLEBERRY FINN*

Huck Finn (whose words are quoted above) experienced a disorienting dilemma. Everything he had been taught told him that he should turn Jim over to the slave catchers and that abolitionists were condemned by God. However, what he learned and what he knew from experience told him not to do it. That kind of dilemma can lead to transformative learning. I want to connect the challenge of learning from the painful past with some current thinking about the way we learn and grow. This work is relevant for understanding how we really can learn from the past, rather than having the past simply reinforce what we think we know or what we wish were true.

Researchers in the field of adult education have been investigating transformative learning, which develops autonomous thinking, since the late 1970s. The transformation refers to changes in a person's frame of reference. A person changes his or her beliefs, attitudes, and emotional reactions through critical reflection about experiences. A major life crisis or transition can trigger a disorienting dilemma, bring about the transformation of one's perspectives, and change one's life. You can probably recall such experiences in your own life.

Educator Jack Mezirow's influential model traces a person's transformation beginning with a disorienting dilemma, followed by rational self-examination and critical assessment of one's assumptions, continuing through several rational analytic steps, and finally ending in the new perspective. Other researchers have broadened the understanding of such transformations by finding that they are more than rational; they are also emotional, creative, and intuitive. Analytic psychology models the mental process of discernment that is needed for such transformation. Discernment calls upon images, symbols, and archetypes as a person becomes receptive to alternative perspectives, recognizes their authenticity, and then, importantly, grieves the loss of old ways of thinking and perceiving.

Both rationality and imagination are integral to creating any new personal vision that makes meaning for one's life experiences. Meaning is constructed from more than knowledge. However, the broader and deeper the knowledge, the deeper the meaning and the richer the life. Such a recognition of our human capacity for learning with both our rationality and intuition recalls the interpretive goals (from chapter 26 on education and outreach) that seek to provide visitors to historic sites the opportunities to form their own intellectual and emotional connections. The ways in which we draw upon and change our ways of thinking recall the ways that cultural imagination and cultural metaphor worked in San Luis de Talimali and early industrial Harpers Ferry.

Educator Melanie Walker describes a democratic society as a "learning society" and explains that learning involves developing not only skills and competencies, but also agency as human beings. She encourages students to learn about themselves and their world but also to develop themselves and contribute to their world. She champions an ethical view of the world that seeks freedom to exercise informed judgment as a vital part of being human. Through her work, she seeks to counter a social environment that encourages passivity, consumerism, and individuality at the expense of social justice and equity.

Walker is an advocate for teaching methods that support the ability for each of us to make choices "in our bid for emotional and intellectual authenticity of the self" (Walker 2001:15). Her questions also are relevant in thinking about providing the opportunities for disorienting dilemmas and transformations in public outreach about lessons gleaned from study of the past.

Transformational learning is not necessarily a matter of teaching per se, but rather of fostering opportunities, such as a learning environment where it is safe to take risks and where there is a community of learners. Walker's work recalls the idea of *ubuntu*, the essential interdependence of human beings of such importance in the operation of the South African Commission of Truth and Reconciliation, as she explains how both teachers and students find identities through each other and through learning communities.

Creating such learning environments can be done in various ways. Educators Michalinos Zembylas and Charalambos Vrasidas discuss a "pedagogy of discomfort" that can offer direction for transformative education through its recognition that effective analysis of ideology requires not only rational inquiry and dialogue but also excavation of the emotional investments that underlie any ideological commitment.... This pedagogy emphasizes the need for both educator and students to move outside of their comfort zones... to leave behind learned beliefs and habits, and enter the risky areas of contradictory and ambiguous ethical and moral differences. (2004:119)

The "dialogues for democracy" used by members of the International Coalition of Historic Site Museums of Conscience comprise one set of methods. The interpretive profession's emphasis on creating opportunities for the "Ah ha—now I get it!" experience and opening up the possibilities for emotional and intellectual connections (rather than insisting on one over the other) is another. Archaeology can offer opportunities for disorienting dilemmas, perhaps by tracing the sources and origins of some of our persistent "isms" based on race, sex, ethnicity, and other factors. Innumerable forms of bigotry exist; most appear to be based on perceptions of entitlement. It can be quite disorienting to realize that one's sense of entitlement or superiority is based on false assumptions, but it is one entry into transformation. Archaeology reveals some of these false assumptions.

My example for this chapter comes from Brazoria, Texas, a small rural community south of Houston that is the site of Levi Jordan's 19th-century sugar plantation. In 1986 Kenneth Brown established a long-term research project on the slave and tenant quarters there. He has uncovered significant data on social and spiritual life and documented the sudden abandonment of tenant housing in the 1880s. The tenants had fled, leaving most of their possessions. Subsequent flooding and silting left the unusually rich archaeological record protected and undisturbed.

A combination of factors led Brown to initiate a public outreach program in 1992. He was anxious to share results from the unusually productive site. In addition, in the late 1980s there were some ugly revelations about violent white supremacist activities of the plantation owners. It became important to try to establish a public conversation about that part of the plantation's history.

Carol McDavid joined the project to establish that outreach. She first conducted an ethnographic project to learn the local social and political landscape and see about the feasibility of local community participation. Specifically, she needed to find out whether people would support and participate in a project which would require them to deal publicly with the ugly and hurtful aspects of Brazoria's history.

McDavid's subsequent work on the public component of the Levi Jordan Plantation project offers an example for the potential of transformative learning, community cooperation, the creation of social capital, confronting a difficult past, and restorative justice. Both black and white descendants were anxious about public association with that history. McDavid describes:

> As the years went on, the project created conflict between family members with different points of view and different tolerances for the expression of multiple truths about the plantation's history. It also, occasionally, created unity where it had not existed before, as members of various descendant groups, many of whom had not previously met, became interested in the archaeological project and began to work on it together. (2004:39)

One of the main tools for community interaction was collaboration on the project's Levi Jordan Plantation website (http://www.webarchaeology.com). This website was created to test the usefulness of the Internet in collaborative community projects, assessing specifically how well it would function to facilitate the kinds of conversation required to confront the difficult past. The website project brought people together to talk about how to share the stories of the plantation's past from the points of view of both black and white descendants.

The project was also transformative for the archaeologist. McDavid (2002:306) describes her experience in giving up some of the authority as an expert (and as a white, urban academic): "When I began to present myself—and, more importantly, to *see* myself—as only one actor in a conversation which allowed space for alternative truth claims, not as someone with a privileged, exclusive way of understanding the past, I began to have more credibility in the community, not less."

The Levi Jordan Plantation Historical Society established some major goals to restore the plantation house, construct a visitor center, and maintain the collaborative website. The project has resulted in state recognition that this property is an extraordinary place to be preserved and commemorated. Texas passed a bond bill to fund the purchase of the property and in 2002 the Texas Parks and Wildlife Department became the new owner. It remains to be seen whether confrontation of the painful past and its legacy will continue within the framework of state ownership, and, if so, how collaborative that process will be.

Related to the possibility of engagement with difficult histories are some insights from Rosenzweig and Thelen's survey, cited in my introduction to this book. Their findings touch upon the possibility of broadening the scope of people's interests beyond family connections to wider communities. The whole human family stands to benefit from connections with the past and with each other through shared history. They write:

> Respondents brooded about this question of whether and under what circumstances individuals could develop a sense of a common past and a common future.... Instead of inheriting or retrieving fully formed collective pasts, individuals felt bursts of recognition when they suddenly felt common points of identity with others in the present that they made into shared experiences and trajectories. Across affiliations, from family to race or religion, from sex or sexual orientation to nation or humanity, individuals experienced moments when they felt more and less connected, more and less alone, when they recognized shared experiences.... Indeed, the changing possibilities for discovering what they shared with others often inspired the most empowering—and discouraging—uses respondents made of the past. (1998:200–201)

The discouraging use of the past they refer to is related to the type of bonding social capital discussed in chapter 29 that can indeed bond members of a group together but also may become dangerous and exclusionary in an "us versus them" sort of way. Zembylas and Vrasidas comment on the potential dangers of such thinking that form in reaction to some historical understandings. One antidote is learning to think critically and being open to learning. They describe how important it is

> to recognize how thinking and feeling define how and what one chooses to see and not to see....It is difficult and painful to examine how some feelings such as anger and indignation...are potentially *mis*-eduative, especially when many individuals find comfort in the solidarities created. (2004:120)

On the other hand, the empowering uses of the past relate to the creation of bridging social capital which acts across social divides to pull people together. Given people's often inward-looking perceptions of history, what is the role of heritage professions in public outreach about the past? The role of social history, whether historical or historical archaeological, is to connect everyday experience to the larger structures of major social change. Historical archaeology can provide, or at least suggest, the connections that individuals and families might not make for themselves. Such a contribution can provide the broad context and the connections that form bridges to others' experiences. Historical archaeology and other heritage professions can help to provide the conceptual spaces in which bridging social capital can develop. It would be widely beneficial to move beyond a history packaged to be of interest only to related groups and move toward an inclusive history where experience is contextualized and people can relate to the lives and histories of others.

Lots of social history, particularly that done in connection with the civil rights and women's liberation movements, was about raising consciousness both within specific groups and in the broader community. By bringing authentic experiences into private and public awareness, these movements challenged assumptions and encouraged changes in perception. Such history was and is based on defensible evidence. Critics may attempt to label such history as "revisionist," by which they imply that it is somehow based solely on desire and political convenience. Historian Eric Foner reminds us that

> [h]istory always has been and always will be regularly rewritten, in response to new questions, new information, new methodologies, and new political, social, and cultural imperatives. But that each generation can and must rewrite history does not mean that history is simply a series of myths and inventions. There are commonly accepted professional standards that enable us to distinguish good history from falsehoods like the denial of the Holocaust. Historical truth does exist, not in the scientific sense but as a reasonable approximation of the past. But the most difficult truth for those outside the ranks of professional historians to accept is that there often exists more than one legitimate way of recounting past events. (2002:xvii)

Archaeologists understand that different perspectives do not create inappropriately chaotic or incomplete views of the past. Instead, as Bruce Trigger (1989:23) explains: "Multiple standpoints...challenge all archaeologists, wherever possible, to use this multiplicity to create more holistic and objective syntheses. Their goal should be an archaeology that is more complete and less biased because it is informed by an ever-increasing number of viewpoints and constrained by more data."

As archaeologists become involved in civic renewal and transformative learning, we will need a discipline that can be of service to society and that offers its scholarship in the public realm. It is important to understand that archaeology's usefulness in support of identity and community does not supercede or override knowledge goals aimed at understanding how things in the past really were. Instead, it relies upon rigorous and defensible scholarship.

CHAPTER 31

Some Closing Thoughts

*The most common way people give up their power is by thinking they don't
have any.*

—ALICE WALKER

The ways in which we pay attention to the past—through research, study,
commemoration, and public interpretation—can indeed transform us.
We can celebrate our history even as we allow it to challenge us to improve
the future.

In the journey of this book I have emphasized questions and questioning as a path of discovery. I have tried to keep the avenues open to find ways
of *sankofa*, of learning from the past—and the ideas we unconsciously and
uncritically accept from the past—so that we might build a compassionate
present. I believe that we all have struggles in common and that our struggles
can unite us across lines we may mistakenly think are etched in stone rather
than drawn in the sand.

I chose the epigraph for this book from James Merrill's extraordinary
poem "Lost in Translation." That's not because I believe historical archaeology is the path to all knowledge or that we really can ever retrieve what is gone.
Loss is indeed one of life's inevitable lessons. Instead I chose it as homage to
the ineffable, to the depth of the ambiguity in which we live and in which we
work to make sense of our lives.

I want to leave this book somewhat open-ended and resist the urge to wrap
up its threads too neatly. You will ultimately decide what you take away from
it and where you go with it. The closing quotes are from the final panels at the
Canadian War Museum in Ottawa (which I visited on August 20, 2005). They
are posted above counters where visitors can write their reflections, comments, and ideas on cards and leave them for the museum staff or take them

away. I took these thoughts away so that I could leave them with you. They speak to our individual and collective power. They speak to our relationship with the past, however we come to understand it, however we come to allow it to transform us.

What do you think?

History is yours. It is not owned or written by someone else for you to learn. It is being made by you, right now, standing in this space, thinking about everything that you have experienced in this museum. It is your rage, your sympathy, your understanding.

What will you do?

History is not just the story you read. It is the one you write. It is the one you remember or denounce or relate to others. It is not predetermined. Every action, every decision, however small, is relevant to its course. History is replete with horror, and replete with hope. You shape the balance.

Further Readings

These readings are suggested in addition to the references that are cited in the text and include my sources. They are not in any sense exhaustive of historical archaeology or other subjects touched upon, but are selected to support or extend points made in the text. For many more examples, see your library catalog. For journals, see especially *Historical Archaeology* and the *International Journal of Historical Archaeology*. Historical archaeology less frequently appears in *American Antiquity, American Anthropologist, World Archaeology,* and other journals. The Society for Historical Archaeology also posts some bibliographies on its website (http://www.sha.org).

1. Do History And Historical Archaeology Matter?

The Henry Ford mission statement
http://www.hfmgv.org/about/mission.asp (accessed July 21, 2006)

Ramos, Maria, and David Duganne
2000   Exploring Public Perceptions and Attitudes about Archaeology. Prepared by Harris Interactive for the Society for American Archaeology. http://www.cr.nps. gov/aad/pubs/Harris/index.htm (accessed July 25, 2005).

Rosenzweig, Roy, and David Thelen
1998   *The Presence of the Past: Popular Uses of History in American Life.* Columbia University Press, New York.

Neal, A. D., and J. L. Martin
2000   *Losing America's Memory: Historical Illiteracy in the 21st Century.* A Report by the American Council of Trustees and Alumni.

➤   *This is one of the many polls about Americans' knowledge of history.*

Little, Barbara J. (editor)
2002   *Public Benefits of Archaeology.* University Press of Florida, Gainesville.

➤   *Archaeologists and nonarchaeologists describe how the field benefits the broader public.*

Chapter 2. The Goals of Historical Archaeology

Shackel, Paul A., and Erve J. Chambers (editors)
2004   *Places in Mind: Public Archaeology as Applied Anthropology.* Routledge, New York.

➤   *See this for case studies on archaeology as applied anthropology.*

Chapter 3. Preserving and Interpreting Sites

Brown, Ralph D.
1937   Archaeological Investigations of the Northwest Company's Post, Grand Portage, Minnesota, 1936. *Indians at Work (OIA).* May 1937.

The Louisbourg Institute
http://collections.ic.gc.ca/louisbourg/enghome.html (accessed August 16, 2006)

Jameson, John H. (editor)
2004   *The Reconstructed Past: Reconstructions in the Public Interpretation of Archaeology.* AltaMira Press, Walnut Creek, CA.

National Park Service
n.d.   Saugus Iron Works: Life and Work at an Early American Industrial Site. Teaching with Historic Places Lesson Plan #30. http://www.cr.nps.gov/nr/twhp/wwwlps/lessons/30saugus/30saugus.htm (accessed July 25, 2006)

Fagan, Brian
2006   *Fish on Friday: Feasting, Fasting, and the Discovery of the New World.* Basic Books, New York.

➤   *Learn about what drove Europe's fishing mania.*

U.S. National Park Service's public website on archaeology
http://www.cr.nps.gov/archeology/public/index.htm (accessed August 16, 2006)

Society for Historical Archaeology
http://www.sha.org (accessed August 16, 2006)

Society for Post-Medieval Archaeology
http://www.asha.org.au

Australasian Society for Historical Archaeology
http://www.asha.org.au (accessed August 16, 2006)

➤   *Learn about how to get involved in archaeology through your state, provincial, or local governments.*

Chapter 4. Rewriting Documentary History

Scott, Douglas D., Richard A. Fox, Jr., Melissa A. Connor, and Dick Harmon
1989   *Archaeological Perspectives on the Battle of the Little Bighorn.* University of Oklahoma Press, Norman.

Fox, Richard A.

1993 *Archaeology, History and Custer's Last Battle: The Little Bighorn Reexamined.* University of Oklahoma Press, Norman.

➤ *Learn about the archaeology at Little Bighorn from the preceding two texts.*

Geier, Clarence R., Jr. and Stephen R. Potter (editors)

2000 *Archaeological Perspectives on the American Civil War.* University Press of Florida, Gainesville.

Greene, Jerome A., and Douglas D. Scott

2004 *Finding Sand Creek: History, Archaeology, and the 1864 Massacre Site.* University of Oklahoma Press, Norman.

➤ *Learn more about battlefield archaeology from the preceding two texts.*

Chapter 5. Reconstructing Ways of Life

Brooks, Meagan

forthcoming Reconnecting the Present with Its Past: The Doukhobor Pit House Public Archaeology Project. In *Archaeology as a Tool of Civic Engagement*, edited by Barbara J. Little and Paul A. Shackel. AltaMira Press, Lanham, MD.

Kozakavich, Stacy C.

2006 Doukhobor Identity and Communalism at Kirilovka Village Site. *Historical Archaeology* 40(1): 119–132.

Lightfoot, K. G., A. M. Schiff, and T. A. Wake (editors)

1997 *The Native Alaskan Neighborhood: A Multi-ethnic community at Fort Ross. The Archaeology and Ethnohistory of Fort Ross, California, vol. 2.* University of California Press, Berkeley.

Veltre, Douglas W., and Allen P. McCartney

2002 Russian Exploitation of Aleuts and Fur Seals: The Archaeology of Eighteenth- and Early Nineteenth-Century Settlements in the Pribilof Islands, Alaska. *Historical Archaeology* 36(3): 8–17.

Crowell, Aron

1997 *Archaeology and the Capitalist World System: A Study from Russian America.* Plenum Press, New York.

➤ *For more about the Russian colonies in North America.*

Chapter 6. Improving Archaeological Methods

Little, Barbara J., Kim Lanphere, and Douglas Owsley

1992 Mortuary Display and Status in a Nineteenth-Century Anglo-American Cemetery in Manassas, Virginia. *American Antiquity* 57(3): 397–418.

McCracken, Grant
1988   *Culture and Consumption: New Approaches to the Symbolic Character of Consumer Goods and Activities*. Indiana University Press, Bloomington.

➤   *Find out more about the "invisible ink" strategy.*

Chapter 7. Understanding Modernization and Globalization

Maniery, Mary L.
2004   The Archaeology of Asian Immigrants: 35 Years in the Making. *The SAA Archaeological Record* 4(5): 10–13.

Voss, Barbara L.
2005   The Archaeology of Overseas Chinese Communities. *World Archaeology* 37(3): 424–439.

Wegars, Priscilla (editor)
1993   *Hidden Heritage: Historical Archaeology of the Overseas Chinese*. Baywood, Amityville, NY.

➤   *Read more about the overseas Chinese in the above readings.*

Faulkner, Alaric, and Gretchen Faulkner
1987   *The French at Pentagoet 1625–1674: An Archaeological Portrait of the Acadian Frontier*. Maine Historic Preservation Commission, Augusta; New Brunswick Museum, St. Johns.

➤   *For one of several examples of some earlier immigrants.*

Chapter 8. A Questioning Attitude

Held, David, and John B. Thompson (editors)
1989   *Social Theory of Modern Societies: Anthony Giddens and His Critics*. Cambridge University Press, Cambridge.

Nader, Laura
2001   Anthropology! Distinguished Lecture—2000. *American Anthropologist* 103(3): 609–620.

Orser, Charles E., Jr.
1996   *A Historical Archaeology of the Modern World*. Plenum Press, New York.

Sahlins, Marshall
1999   What Is Anthropological Enlightenment? Some Lessons of the Twentieth Century. *Annual Review of Anthropology* 28:i–xxii.

Funari, Pedro P., Martin Hall, and Sian Jones (editors)
1999   *Historical Archaeology: Back from the Edge*. Routledge, London.

Little, Barbara J. (editor)
1992   *Text-Aided Archeology.* CRC Press, Boca Raton, Florida.

➤   *The two preceding collections take a broad view of historical archaeology.*

Adonis
1990   *An Introduction to Arab Poetics.* Translated from the Arabic by Catherine Cobham. Saqi Books, London.

➤   *This sounds like an unlikely recommended reading for an archaeology book, but try it, particularly if you want an entirely different view on what "modern" means.*

Chapter 9. Defining Our Topics

Hardesty, Donald L., Steven F. Mehls, Edward J. Stoner, and Monique E. Kimball
1994   *Riepetown: A Data Recovery Report for the Historic Townsite of Riepetown, White Pine County, Nevada.* Report prepared for Magma Copper Company by Western Cultural Resource Management, Sparks, Nevada.

Ludlow Collective
2002   The Colorado Coal Field War Archaeology Project. *The SAA Archaeological Record* 2(2): 21–23. http://www.saa.org/Publications/theSAAarchRec/mar02.pdf (accessed July 25, 2006)

Rogge, A. Eugene, D. L. McWatters, M. Keane, and R. Emanuel
1995   *Raising Arizona's Dams: Daily Life, Danger, and Discrimination in the Dam Construction Camps of Central Arizona, 1890s–1940s.* University of Arizona Press, Tucson.

Van Bueren, Thad
2002   Struggling with Class Relations at a Los Angeles Aqueduct Construction Camp. *Historical Archaeology* 36(3): 28–43.

Buchli, Victor, and Gavin Lucas (editors)
2001   *Archaeologies of the Contemporary Past.* Routledge, New York.

Shanks, Michael
1992   *Experiencing the Past.* Routledge, London.

➤   *The two preceding books will give you a sense of contemporary uses of archaeology.*

Leone, Mark P., and Parker B. Potter, Jr. (editors)
1999   *Historical Archaeologies of Capitalism.* Kluwer, New York.

Orser, Charles E., Jr.
1996   *A Historical Archaeology of the Modern World.* Plenum Press, New York.

Orser, Charles E., Jr. (editor)
2001   *Race and the Archaeology of Identity.* University of Utah Press, Salt Lake City.

Patterson, Thomas C.
1995   *Toward a Social History of Archaeology in the United States*. Harcourt Brace and Company, Fort Worth, TX.

>   *For more about the social context of archaeology as a whole.*

Chapter 10. Colonialism, Capitalism, and Slavery

Andrews, Susan C., and James P. Fenton
2001   Archaeology and the Invisible Man: The Role of Slavery in the Production of Wealth and Social Class in the Bluegrass Region of Kentucky, 1820 to 1870. *World Archaeology* 33(1): 115–135.

Rubertone, Patricia
2001   *Grave Undertakings: An Archaeology of Roger Williams and the Narragansett Indians*. Smithsonian Institution Press, Washington, DC.

Rubertone, Patricia
2000   The Historical Archaeology of Native Americans. *Annual Review of Anthropology* 29:425–446.

Ramenofsky, Ann
1987   *Vectors of Death: The Archaeology of European Contact*. University of New Mexico Press, Albuquerque.

>   *For more about the biological impact of contact.*

Fitzhugh, William W., and Jacqueline S. Olin (editors)
1993   *Archaeology of the Frobisher Voyages*. Smithsonian Institution Press, Washington, DC.

>   *For more about archaeology of exploration.*

Comer, Douglas C.
1996   *Ritual Ground: Bent's Old Fort, World Formation, and the Annexation of the Southwest*. University of California Press, Berkeley.

Dawdy, Shannon Lee (editor)
2000   Creolization. *Historical Archaeology* 34(4).

Ewen, Charles R.
1991   *From Spaniard to Creole: The Archaeology of Cultural Formation at Puerto Real, Haiti*. University of Alabama Press, Tuscaloosa.

McEwan, Bonnie G., and Gregory A. Waselkov (editors)
2003   Colonial Origins: The Archaeology of Colonialism in the Americas. *Historical Archaeology* 37(4).

Thomas, David Hurst (editor)
1989   *Columbian Consequences. Vol. 1. Archaeological and Historical Perspectives on the Spanish Borderlands West*. Smithsonian Institution Press, Washington, DC.

1990   *Columbian Consequences. Vol. 2. Archaeological and Historical Perspectives on the Spanish Borderlands East.* Smithsonian Institution Press, Washington, DC.

1991   *Columbian Consequences. Vol. 3. The Spanish Borderlands in Pan-American Perspective.* Smithsonian Institution Press, Washington, DC.

➤   *For more about colonialism and creolization see the readings above.*

Chapter 11. What Is Our Evidence?

Walsh, Lorena S., Ann Smart Martin, and Joanne Bowen

1997   "Provisioning Early American Towns. The Chesapeake: A Multidisciplinary Case Study," final performance report for the National Endowment for the Humanities Grant RO-22643-93. An online version of report is available: http://research history.org/Archaeological_Research/Research_Articles/ThemeZooarch/Provisioning.cfm (accessed August 16, 2006).

Young, Amy L., Michael Tuma, and Cliff Jenkins

2001   The Role of Hunting to Cope with Risk at Saragossa Plantation, Natchez, Mississippi. *American Anthropologist* 103(3): 692–704.

Lubar, Steven, and W. David Kingery (editors)

1993   *History from Things: Essays on Material Culture.* Smithsonian Institution Press, Washington, DC.

Miller, Daniel

1987   *Material Culture and Mass Consumption.* Blackwell, Oxford.

Noel Hume, Ivor

1969   *A Guide to Artifacts of Colonial America.* Random House, New York.

➤   *There are a lot of really interesting books about material culture. The preceding three are just a couple. Also take a look at the* Winterthur Portfolio, *a Journal of American Material Culture, and publications from Winterthur.*

Pearson, Marlys, and Paul R. Mullins

1999   Domesticating Barbie: An Archaeology of Barbie Material Culture and Domestic Ideology. *International Journal of Historical Archaeology* 3(4): 225–259.

➤   *Take a look at this one for something you might not expect to see.*

Chapter 12. Ideology, Ambiguity, and Muted Groups

Brashler, Janet G.

1991   When Daddy Was a Shanty Boy: The Role of Gender in the Organization of the Logging Industry in Highland West Virginia. *Historical Archaeology* 25(4): 54–68.

Kryder-Reid, Elizabeth

1994   "With Manly Courage": Reading the Construction of Gender in a 19th-Century Religious Community. In *Those of Little Note: Gender, Race and Class in*

Historical Archaeology, edited by Elizabeth M. Scott, pp. 97–114. University of Arizona Press, Tucson.

Little, Barbara J.
1997   Expressing Ideology without a Voice, or, Obfuscation and the Enlightenment. *International Journal of Historical Archaeology* 1(3): 225–241.

Burley, David V.
1989   Function, Meaning and Context: Ambiguities in Ceramic Use by the Hivernant Metis of the Northwest Plains. *Historical Archaeology* 23(1): 97–106.

➤   *For more about the ambiguity of interpreting ceramics.*

Wolf, Eric
1990   Distinguished Lecture: Facing Power—Old Insights, New Questions. *American Anthropologist* 92(3): 586–596.

➤   *For more about power and ideology.*

Chapter 13. Ethical Considerations

Brodie, N., J. Doole, and C. Renfrew (editors)
2001   *Trade in Illicit Antiquities: The Destruction of the World's Archaeological Heritage.* McDonald Institute, Cambridge.

Childs, S. Terry
2004   *Our Collective Responsibility: The Ethics and Practice of Archaeological Collections Stewardship.* Society for American Archaeology, Washington, DC.

Thomas, David Hurst
2000   *Skull Wars: Kennewick Man, Archaeology, and the Battle for Native American Identity.* Basic Books, New York.

Zimmerman, Larry J., Karen D. Vitelli, and Julie Hollowell-Zimmer (editors)
2003   *Ethical Issues in Archaeology.* Published in cooperation with the Society for American Archaeology, AltaMira Press, Walnut Creek, CA.

➤   *In addition to the ethics statements of professional organizations, see the preceding texts.*

Hardesty, Donald L., and Barbara J. Little
2000   *Assessing Site Significance: A Guide for Archaeologists and Historians.* AltaMira Press, Walnut Creek, CA.

➤   *Learn more about the concept of significance in cultural resource management.*

Saving Antiquities for Everyone (SAFE)
http://www.savingantiquities.org/index.htm (accessed August 16, 2006)

➤   *SAFE is an organization dedicated to preservation.*

Section 3: A Windshield Survey of Historical Archaeology

> ➤ *There are a lot of books and journals about particular sites, regions, or themes that will give you a much more thorough look at the field. I can't begin to list them. However, take a look at this one:*

De Cunzo, Lu Ann, and John H. Jameson, Jr. (editors)
2005 *Unlocking the Past: Celebrating Historical Archaeology in North America.* University Press of Florida, Gainesville.

Chapter 14. Introduction to a Windshield Survey of Historical Archaeology

Wilkie, Laurie A.
2000 *Creating Freedom: Material Culture and African American Identity at Oakley Plantation, Louisiana, 1840–1950.* Louisiana State University Press, Baton Rouge.

> ➤ *I created the image of the Gulf Coast archaeologist from Laurie Wilkie, so it seems only fair to cite one of her books.*

Chapter 15. The Survival of the English Colony at Jamestown

Hantman, Jeffrey L.
1990 Between Powhatan and Quirank: Reconstructing Monacan Culture and History in the Context of Jamestown. *American Anthropologist* 92(1): 676–690.
2004 Monacan Meditation: Regional and Individual Archaeologies in the Contemporary Politics of Indian Heritage. In *Places in Mind: Public Archaeology as Applied Anthropology,* edited by Paul A. Shackel and Erve J. Chambers, pp. 19–33. Routledge, New York.

APVA Jamestown Rediscovery
http://www.apva.org/jr.html (accessed October 10, 2005)

Kelso, William M., and Jamestown Rediscovery Team
2000 *Jamestown Rediscovery: Search for the 1607 James Fort.* University Press of Virginia, Charlottesville.

Noel Hume, Ivor, and Audrey Noel Hume
2001 *The Archaeology of Martin's Hundred,* 2 vols. Colonial Williamsburg Foundation.

Stahle, David W., Malcolm K. Cleveland, Dennis B. Blanton, Matthew D. Therrell, and David A. Gay
1998 The Jamestown and Lost Colony Droughts. *Science* 280 (S363): 564–567.

Chapter 16. Mission San Luis de Talimali

Ewen, Charles R.
1996 Continuity and Change: De Soto and the Apalachee. *Historical Archaeology* 30(2): 41–53.

Gentleman from Elvas
1993   The Account of the Gentleman from Elvas, translated by J. Robertson and J. Hann. In *The De Soto Chronicles, Vol. 1*, edited by Lawrence Clayton, Vernon J. Knight, and Edward Moore, pp. 19–220. University of Alabama Press, Tuscaloosa.

Graham, Elizabeth
1998   Mission Archaeology. *Annual Review of Anthropology* 27:25–62.

McEwan, Bonnie G.
2001   The Spiritual Conquest of La Florida. *American Anthropologist* 103(3): 633–644.

McEwan, Bonnie G., and John H. Hann
2000   Reconstructing a Spanish Mission: San Luis de Talimali. *OAH Magazine of History* 14 (Summer).

Deagan, Kathleen A.
1983   *Spanish St. Augustine: The Archaeology of a Colonial Creole Community.* Academic Press, New York.

➤ *Find out more about the Spanish in North America (and see some of the recommendations under colonialism above too). You'll run across Kathy Deagan's work a lot if you're interested in the southeast, including the Caribbean. Start with this classic.*

Deagan, Kathleen A.
1996   Colonial Transformation: Euro-American Cultural Genesis in the Early Spanish-American Colonies. *Journal of Anthropological Research* 522:154.

Historical archaeology at the Florida Museum of Natural History
St. Augustine: America's ancient city
http://www.flmnh.ufl.edu/histarch/StAugustine.htm (accessed August 16, 2006)

➤ *St. Augustine is also a major tourist draw. Take a look at the online exhibits, as well as artifact catalogs.*

Milanich, Jerald T.
1999 *Laboring in the Fields of the Lord: Spanish Missions and Southeastern Indians.* Smithsonian Institution Press, Washington, DC.

South, Stanley
1991 *Archaeology at Santa Elena: Doorway to the Past.* South Carolina Institute of Archaeology and Anthropology, Columbia.

Chapter 17. Enclosure of the English Countryside

Johnson, Matthew
1996   *An Archaeology of Capitalism.* Blackwell, Oxford.

Shackel, Paul A.
1993   *Personal Discipline and Material Culture: An Archaeology of Annapolis, Maryland, 1695–1870.* University of Tennessee Press, Knoxville.

Williamson, Tom
1998   Gentry Landscapes in a Much Older Land. *British Archaeology* 36.

Tarlow, Sarah, and Susie West (editors)
1999   *The Familiar Past? Archaeologies of Later Historical Britain.* Routledge, London.

➤   *For more about England.*

Chapter 18. Capitalism, the Georgian Order, and a Woman

Deetz, James
1977   *In Small Things Forgotten: The Archaeology of Early American Life.* Doubleday, New York.

Little, Barbara J.
1994   "She was…an Example to her Sex": Possibilities for a Feminist Historical Archaeology. In *The Historical Archaeology of the Chesapeake*, edited by Paul A. Shackel and Barbara J. Little, pp. 189–204. Smithsonian Institution Press, Washington, DC.

Markell, Ann, Martin Hall, and Carmel Schrire
1995   The Historical Archaeology of Vergelehen, an Early Farmstead at the Cape of Good Hope. *Historical Archaeology* 29(1): 10–34.

Wall, Diana diZerega
1994   *The Archaeology of Gender: Separating the Spheres in Urban America.* Plenum Press, New York.

➤   *For more about relationships between gender ideology and things.*

Chapter 19. Australia's Convict Past

Casella, Eleanor Conlin
2001   Every Procurable Object: A Functional Analysis of the Ross Factory Archaeological Collections. *Australian Historical Archaeology* 19:25–38.
2005   Prisoner of His Majesty: Postcoloniality and the Archaeology of British Penal Transportation. *World Archaeology* 37(3): 453–467.

Connah, Graham
2001   The Lake Innes Estate: Privilege and Servitude in Nineteenth-Century Australia. *World Archaeology* 33(1): 137–154.

Gallop, Geoff
2001   Speech. John Boyle O'Reilly Commemoration ceremony. March 25, 2001.
Western Australia. http://www.premier.wa.gov.au/docs/speeches/JohnBoyleOreilly
CommemorationLeschenaultPenin250301.pdf (accessed 15 June 2006)

Colley, Sarah
2002   *Uncovering Australia: Archaeology, Indigenous People and the Public.* Smithsonian Institution Press, Washington, DC.

Connah, Graham
1988   *The Archaeology of Australia's History.* Cambridge University Press, Cambridge.

➤ *For more about Australia, see the preceding two texts.*

Chapter 20. Archaeology of African American Life

Singleton, Theresa A. (editor)
1999   *"I, Too, Am America": Archaeological Studies of African American Life.* University of Virginia Press, Charlottesville.

➤ *Start with this one. In it you will find the arguments about Chesapeake pipes (see the chapters by Matthew Emerson and by this long list of authors who take exception to it: Daniel Mouer, Mary Ellen Hodges, Stephen Potter, Susan Henry Renaud, Ivor Noel Hume, Dennis Pogue, Martha McCartney, and Thomas Davidson). You'll also find a reprint of James Deetz's influential 1988 article from* Science *and lots more.*

Ferguson, Leland
1992   *Uncommon Ground: The Archaeology of African America, 1650–1800.* Smithsonian Institution Press, Washington, DC.

➤ *I'd say this one is a must-read.*

Ferguson, Leland
1991   Struggling with Pots in Colonial South Carolina. In *The Archaeology of Inequality,* edited by Randall H. McGuire and Robert Paynter. Blackwell, Oxford.

Blakey, Michael
2001   Bioarchaeology of the African Diaspora in the Americas: Its Origins and Scope. *Annual Review of Anthropology* 30:387–422.

➤ *For a good overview of African American vindicationist scholarship and many early references, start with this one.*

Weik, Terry
1997   The Archaeology of Maroon Societies in the Americas: Resistance, Cultural Continuity and Transformation in the African Diaspora. *Historical Archaeology* 31(2): 81–92.

➤ *For more on maroon settlements.*

Funari, Pedro Paulo A.

1995 The Archaeology of Palmares and its Contribution to the Understanding of the History of African American Culture. *Historical Archaeology in Latin America* 7:1–41.

2006 Conquistadors, Plantations, and Quilombo: Latin America in Historical Archaeological Context. In *Historical Archaeology*, edited by Martin Hall and Stephen W. Silliman, pp. 209–229. Blackwell, Oxford.

> *For more on Palmares (you'll also find more in Orser's 1996 book,* A Historical Archaeology of the Modern World, *recommended above).*

Mullins, Paul R.

2006 Racializing the Commonplace Landscape: An Archaeology of Urban Renewal Along the Color Line. *World Archaeology* 38(1): 60–71.

New Philadelphia archaeology program

http://www.heritage.umd.edu/CHRSWeb/New%20Philadelphia/NewPhiladelphia. htm (accessed October 10, 2005)

Wall, Diana diZerega, Nan A. Rothschild, Cynthia Copeland, and Herbert Seignoret

2004 The Seneca Village Project: Working with Modern Communities in Creating the Past. In *Places in Mind: Public Archaeology as Applied Anthropology*, edited by Paul A. Shackel and Erve J. Chambers, pp. 101–117. Routledge, New York.

Yates Community Archaeology Project

http://www.publicarchaeology.org/yates/history.html (accessed April 6, 2006)

Franklin, Maria, and Larry McKee (editors)

2004 African Diasporic Archaeologies. *Historical Archaeology* 38(1).

Leone, Mark P., Cheryl Janifer LaRoche, and Jennifer J. Babiarz

2005 The Archaeology of Black Americans in Recent Times. *Annual Review of Anthropology* 34:574–598.

Mullins, Paul R.

1999 *Race and Affluence: An Archaeology of African American and Consumer Culture.* Klewer Academic/Plenum Press, New York.

Cottman, M. H.

1999 *The Wreck of the Henrietta Marie: An African-American's Spiritual Journey to Uncover a Sunken Slave Ship's Past.* Harmony, New York.

> *You will be interested to read about this underwater site, which had the misfortune to have been found by the infamous Mel Fisher and the good fortune to have been championed by the National Association of Black Scuba Divers.*

African Diaspora Archaeology Network

http://www.diaspora.uiuc.edu (accessed October 10, 2005)

> *You can keep up with some of this research and more online.*

The Digital Archaeological Archive of Comparative Slavery

http://www.daacs.org (accessed February 3, 2006)

Chapter 21. The Machine in the Garden

Johnson, Mark
1987   *The Body in the Mind: The Bodily Basis of Meaning, Imagination, and Reason.* University of Chicago Press, Chicago.

Lakoff, George
1987   *Women, Fire, and Dangerous Things: What Categories Reveal About the Mind.* University of Chicago Press, Chicago.

Marx, Leo
1964   *The Machine in the Garden: Technology and the Pastoral Ideal in America.* Oxford University Press, New York.

Shackel, Paul A.
1996   *Culture Change and the New Technology: An Archaeology of the Early American Industrial Era.* Plenum Press, New York.

Palus, Matthew M., and Paul A. Shackel
2006   *They Worked Regular: Craft, Labor, and Family in the Industrial Community of Virginius Island.* University of Tennessee Press, Knoxville.

➤ *For more about the Harpers Ferry area.*

Mrowzowski, Stephen A., Grace H. Ziesing, and Mary C. Beaudry
1996   *Living on the Boott: Historical Archaeology at the Boott Mills Boardinghouses, Lowell, Massachusetts.* University of Massachusetts Press, Amherst.

Gordon, Robert B. and Patrick Malone
1994   *The Texture of Industry: An Archaeological View of the Industrialization of North America.* Oxford University Press, New York.

➤ *Here are two other books related to industry.*

Chapter 22. The Inner-City Working Class

Yamin, Rebecca (editor)
2001   Becoming New York: The Five Points Neighborhood. *Historical Archaeology* 35(3).

The Five Points Site
http://r2.gsa.gov/fivept/fphome.htm (accessed August 16, 2006)

➤ *Archaeologists and historians rediscover a famous New York City neighborhood.*

Cheek, Charles D., and Amy Friedlander
1990   Pottery and Pig's Feet: Space, Ethnicity and Neighborhood in Washington, DC, 1880–1940. *Historical Archaeology* 24(1): 34–60.

Little, Barbara J., and Nancy J. Kassner
2002   Archaeology in the Alleys of Washington, DC. In *The Archaeology of Urban Landscapes: Explorations in Slumland*, edited by Alan Mayne and Tim Murray, pp. 57–68. Cambridge University Press, Cambridge.

McDaniel, George William
1979   Preserving the People's History: Traditional Black Material Culture in Nineteenth and Twentieth-Century Southern Maryland. Ph.D. dissertation, Duke University.

➤   *On Washington, DC.*

Praetzellis, Mary, and Adrian Praetzellis (editors)
2004   *Putting the "There" There: Historical Archaeologies of West Oakland.* I-880 Cypress Freeway Replacement Project. Anthropological Studies Center, Sonoma State University. California Department of Transportation contract 04A0538, Task Order 15. http://www.sonoma.edu/asc/cypress/finalreport/index.htm (accessed June 15, 2006)

➤   *On West Oakland.*

Mayne, Alan, and Tim Murray (editors)
2001   *The Archaeology of Urban Landscapes: Explorations in Slumland.* Cambridge University Press, Cambridge.

➤   *About the archaeology of inner cities across the globe.*

Chapter 23. Garbage and Garbage-in-Waiting

Majewski, Teresita, and Michael Brian Schiffer
2001   Beyond Consumption: Toward an Archaeology of Consumerism. In *Archaeologies of the Contemporary Past*, edited by Victor Buchli and Gavin Lucas, pp. 26–50. Routledge, New York.

Rathje, William L.
2001   Integrated Archaeology: A Garbage Paradigm. In *Archaeologies of the Contemporary Past*, edited by Victor Buchli and Gavin Lucas, pp. 63–76. Routledge, New York.

Rathje, William L., and C. Murphy
1992   *Rubbish! The Archaeology of Garbage.* Harper Collins, New York.

The Center for a New American Dream
http://www.newdream.org (accessed August 16, 2006)

➤   *Here's something worth thinking about as you consider consumerism: The Center for a New American Dream's mission is to help Americans consume responsibly to protect the environment, enhance quality of life, and promote social justice.*

Chapter 24. Introduction to Public Archaeology

Graubard, Stephen R.
2004   Public Scholarship: A New Perspective for the 21st Century. Carnegie Corpo-
ration of New York. Electronic document, www.carnegie.org/pdf/carnegie_txt.pdf
(accessed December 1, 2005)

Derry, Linda, and Maureen Malloy (editors)
2003   *Archaeologists and Local Communities: Partners in Exploring the Past.* Society for
American Archaeology, Washington, DC.

➤   *For more about public archaeology.*

Chapter 25. Public Memory and Public Places

Bruner, Edward M.
1996   Tourism in Ghana: The Representation of Slavery and the Return of the Black
Diaspora. *American Anthropologist* 98(2):   290–304.

National Park Service National Heritage Areas
http://www.cr.nps.gov/heritageareas (accessed October 10, 2005).

DeCorse, Christopher R.
2001   *An Archaeology of Elmina: Africans and Europeans on the Gold Coast, 1400–
1900.* Smithsonian Institution Press, Washington, DC.

➤   *Learn about the archaeology at the site of Elmina surrounding the castle and
dungeons.*

Jameson, John H. (editor)
1997   *Presenting Archaeology to the Public: Digging for Truths.* AltaMira Press, Walnut
Creek, CA.

➤   *For more on public commemoration and presentation.*

Potter, Parker B., Jr
1994   *Public Archaeology in Annapolis: A Critical Approach to History in Maryland's
Ancient City.* Smithsonian Institution Press, Washington, DC.

Shackel, Paul A.
2000   *Archaeology and Created Memory: Public History in a National Park.* Kluwer
Academic/Plenum Press, New York.
2003   *Memory in Black and White: Race, Commemoration, and the Post-Bellum Landscape.* AltaMira Press, Walnut Creek, CA.

Shackel, Paul A. (editor)
2001   *Myth, Memory, and the Making of the American Landscape.* University Press of
Florida, Gainesville.

Rowan, Yorke, and Uzi Baram (editors)
2004 *Marketing Heritage: Archaeology and the Consumption of the Past.* AltaMira Press, Walnut Creek, CA.

Chapter 26. Education and Outreach

Morrell, David
2002 *Lessons from a Lifetime of Writing: A Novelist Looks at His Craft.* Writer's Digest Books, Cincinnati, OH.

➤ *This is where I learned about the difference between a story and a plot.*

National Association for Interpretation
http://www.interpnet.com (accessed October 10, 2005).

Praetzellis, Adrian
1998 Introduction: Why Every Archaeologist Should Tell Stories Once in a While. *Historical Archaeology* 32(1): 1–3.

Spector, Janet D.
1993 *What This Awl Means: Feminist Archaeology at a Wahpeton Dakota Village.* Minnesota Historical Society, St. Paul.

Smardz, Karolyn, and Shelley J. Smith (editors)
2000 *The Archaeological Education Handbook: Sharing the Past with Kids.* AltaMira Press, Walnut Creek, CA.

➤ *Learn more about how archaeologists work in the K–12 classroom.*

Chapter 27. What About the Painful Past?

United States Institute of Peace Truth Commissions Digital Collection
http://www.usip.org/library/truth.html (accessed February 3, 2006)

African Burial Ground
http://www.africanburialground.gov/ABG_Main.htm (accessed June 15, 2006)

➤ *The final reports on archaeology, history, skeletal biology, and memorialization are available here.*

Chapter 28. History and the Culture Wars

Nash, Gary B., Charlotte Crabtree, and Ross E. Dunn
1998 *History on Trial: Culture Wars and the Teaching of the Past.* Alfred A. Knopf, New York.

Linenthal, Edward T., and Tom Engelhardt (editors)
1996 *History Wars: The Enola Gay and Other Battles for the American Past.* Metropoli-
tan Books, New York.

Schlesinger, Arthur M., Jr.
1992 *The Disuniting of America: Reflections on a Multicultural Society.* W.W. Norton
and Company, New York.

Chapter 29. Civic Renewal and Restorative Justice

Orser, Charles E., Jr.
2004 Archaeological Interpretation and the Irish Diasporic Community. In *Places in
Mind: Public Archaeology as Applied Anthropology*, edited by Paul A. Shackel and
Erve J. Chambers, pp. 171–191. Routledge, New York.

Little, Barbara J., and Paul A. Shackel (editors)
forthcoming *Archaeology as a Tool of Civic Engagement.* AltaMira Press, Lanham, MD.

BetterTogether, an initiative of the Saguaro Seminar: Civic Engagement in America at
Harvard University
http://www.bettertogether.org (accessed February 3, 2006)

➤ *Learn more about social capital and civic renewal.*

International Coalition of Historic Site Museums of Conscience
http://www.sitesofconscience.org (accessed October 10, 2005)

Bohm, David
1996 *On Dialogue.* Routledge, New York.

Yankelovoich, Daniel
1999 *The Magic of Dialogue: Transforming Conflict into Cooperation.* Simon & Schus-
ter, New York.

National Coalition for Dialogue and Deliberation
http://thataway.org/index.html (accessed October 10, 2005)

➤ *See the preceding three texts to learn about dialogue techniques.*

Chapter 30. Transformative Learning

Boyd, Robert D., and J. Gordon Myers
1988 Transformative Education. *International Journal of Lifelong Education* 7(4):
261–284.

Brown, Kenneth L.
1994 Material Culture and Community Structure: The Slave and Tenant Community at Levi Jordan's Plantation, 1848–1892. In *Working Toward Freedom: Slave*

Society and Domestic Economy in the American South, edited by Larry E. Hudson, Jr. pp. 95–118. University of Rochester Press, Rochester, NY.

McDavid, Carol

2002 Archaeologies That Hurt; Descendants That Matter: A Pragmatic Approach to Collaboration in the Public Interpretation of African-American Archaeology. *World Archaeology* 34(2): 303–314.

2004 From "Traditional" Archaeology to Public Archaeology to Community Action: The Levi Jordan Plantation Project. In *Places in Mind: Public Archaeology as Applied Anthropology*, edited by Paul A. Shackel and Erve J. Chambers, pp. 35–56. Routledge, New York.

Mezirow, Jack

1991 *Transformative Dimensions of Adult Learning*. Jossey-Bass, San Francisco.

Walker, Melanie

2001 Higher Education, Critical Professionalism and Educational Action Research. *Debates in Higher Education*, University College London. Electronic document, http://www.ucl.ac.uk/cishe/seminars/dhe_papers/MWpaper.doc (accessed July 25, 2005)

Zembylas, Michalinos, and Charalambos Vrasidas

2004 Emotion, Reason, and Information and Communication Technologies in Education: Some Issues in a Post-Emotional Society. *E-Learning* 1(1): 105–127.

References Cited

Appleby, Joyce, Lynne Hunt, and Margaret Jacob
1995   *Telling the Truth about History*. W. W. Norton and Company, New York.

Barrett, Brenda, and Augie Carlino
2003   What Is in the Future for the Heritage Area Movement? *Forum Journal* 17(4): 51–56.

Blakey, Michael
2004   Introduction. In *The New York African Burial Ground Skeletal Biology Final Report, Vol. I*, edited by M. Blakey and L. Rankin-Hill, pp. 2–37. The African Burial Ground Project, Howard University, Washington, DC, for the United States General Services Administration, Northeast and Caribbean Region. Electronic document, http://www. africanburialground.gov/ABG_FinalReports.htm, accessed July 25, 2005.

Blakey, M. L., L. M. Rankin-Hill, J. E. Howson, and S. H. H. Carrington
2004   The Political Economy of Forced Migration: Sex Ratios, Mortality, Population Growth and Fertility among Africans in Colonial New York. In *The New York African Burial Ground Skeletal Biology Final Report, Vol. I*, edited by M. Blakey and L. Rankin-Hill, pp. 514–540. The African Burial Ground Project, Howard University, Washington, DC, for the United States General Services Administration, Northeast and Caribbean Region. Electronic document, http://www.africanburial-ground.gov/ABG_FinalReports.htm, accessed July 25, 2005.

Bograd, Mark D., and Theresa A. Singleton
1997   The Interpretation of Slavery: Mount Vernon, Monticello, and Colonial Williamsburg. In *Presenting Archaeology to the Public: Digging for Truths*, edited by John H. Jameson. AltaMira Press, Walnut Creek, CA.

Borchert, James
1982   *Alley Life in Washington: Family, Community, Religion and Folklife in the City, 1850–1970*. University of Illinois Press, Chicago.

Brumfiel, Elizabeth M.
2003   It's a Material World: History, Artifacts, and Anthropology. *Annual Review of Anthropology* 32:205–223.

Bruner, Edward M.
1996   Tourism in Ghana; The Representation of Slavery and the Return of the Black Diaspora. *American Anthropologist* 98(2): 290–304.

Cabak, Melanie A., and Mary M. Inkrot
1997   Old Farm, New Farm: An Archaeology of Rural Modernization in the Aiken
       Plateau, 1875–1950. Savannah River Archaeological Research Paper No. 9. Occa-
       sional Papers of the Savannah River Archaeological Research Program, South Car-
       olina Institute of Archaeology and Anthropology, University of South Carolina.

Casella, Eleanor Conlin
2005   Prisoner of His Majesty: Postcoloniality and the Archaeology of British Penal
       Transportation. World Archaeology 37(3): 453–467.

Chappell, Edward A.
1989   Social Responsibility and the American History Museum. Winterthur Portfolio
       24:265.

Connah, Graham
2001   The Lake Innes Estate: Privilege and Servitude in Nineteenth-Century Austra-
       lia. World Archaeology 33(1): 137–154.

Costello, Julia G.
2004   The Chinese in Gum San ("Golden Mountain"). The SAA Archaeological
       Record 4(5): 14–17.

Deagan, Kathleen A., and Jane Landers
1999   Fort Mose: Earliest Free African-American Town in the United States. In I,
       Too, Am America: Archaeological Studies of African-American Life, edited by T. A.
       Singleton, pp. 261–282. University Press of Virginia, Charlottesville.

Deetz, James
1991   Introduction. In Historical Archaeology in Global Perspective, edited by Lisa
       Falk, pp. 1–9. Smithsonian Institution Press, Washington, DC.

Diamant, Rolf
2000   From Management to Stewardship: The Making and Remaking of the U.S.
       National Park System. The George Wright Forum 17(2): 31–45.

Federal Writer's Project
1937   Washington: City and Capital. American Guide Series, Washington, DC.

Fee, Jeffrey M.
1993   Idaho's Chinese Mountain Gardens. In Hidden Heritage: Historical Archaeol-
       ogy of the Overseas Chinese, edited by P. Wegars, pp. 65–96. Baywood, Amityville,
       NY.

Foner, Eric
2002   Who Owns History? Rethinking the Past in a Changing World. Hill and Wang,
       New York.

Ferguson, Leland
1992   Uncommon Ground: The Archaeology of African America, 1650–1800. Smithso-
       nian Institution Press, Washington, DC.

Gallop, Geoff

2001 Speech. John Boyle O'Reilly Commemoration ceremony. March 25, 2001. Western Australia. Electronic document, http://www.premier.wa.gov.au/docs/ speeches/JohnBoyleOreillyCommemorationLeschenaultPenin250301.pdf, accessed June 15, 2006.

Gentleman from Elvas

1993 The Account of the Gentleman from Elvas, translated by J. Robertson and J. Hann. In *The De Soto Chronicles, Vol. I*, edited by Lawrence Clayton, Vernon J. Knight, and Edward Moore, pp. 19–220. University of Alabama Press, Tuscaloosa.

Gilchrist, Roberta

2005 Introduction: Scales and Voices in World Historical Archaeology. *World Archaeology* 37(3): 329–336.

Graham, Elizabeth

1998 Mission Archaeology. *Annual Review of Anthropology* 27:25–62.

Hantman, Jeffrey L.

1990 Between Powhatan and Quirank: Reconstructing Monacan Culture and History in the Context of Jamestown. *American Anthropologist* 92(1): 676–690.

Kozakavich, Stacy C.

2006 Doukhobor Identity and Communalism at Kirilovka Village Site. *Historical Archaeology* 40(1): 119–132.

LaRoche, Cheryl J., and Michael L. Blakey

1997 Seizing Intellectual Power: The Dialogue at the New York African Burial Ground. *Historical Archaeology* 31(3): 84–106.

Lowenthal, David

1998 *The Heritage Crusade and the Spoils of History*. Cambridge University Press, Cambridge.

Majewski, Teresita, and Michael Brian Schiffer

2001 Beyond Consumption: Toward an Archaeology of Consumerism. In *Archaeologies of the Contemporary Past*, edited by Victor Buchli and Gavin Lucas, pp. 26–50. Routledge, New York.

McDavid, Carol

2002 Archaeologies That Hurt; Descendants That Matter: A Pragmatic Approach to Collaboration in the Public Interpretation of African-American Archaeology. *World Archaeology* 34(2): 303–314.

McDavid, Carol

2004 From "Traditional" Archaeology to Public Archaeology to Community Action: The Levi Jordan Plantation Project. In *Places in Mind: Public Archaeology as Applied Anthropology*, edited by Paul A. Shackel and Erve J. Chambers, pp. 35–56. Routledge, New York.

McGuire, Randall
2003   Foreword. In *Ethical Issues in Archaeology,* edited by L. J. Zimmerman, K. D. Vitelli, and J. Hollowell-Zimmer, pp. vii–ix. Published in cooperation with the Society for American Archaeology, AltaMira Press, Walnut Creek, CA.

McManamon, Francis P.
1996   The Antiquities Act—Setting Basic Preservation Policies. *CRM* 19(7): 18–23.

Metcalf, Fay
2002   Myths, Lies, and Videotapes: Information as Antidote to Social Studies Classrooms and Pop Culture. In *Public Benefits of Archaeology*, edited by Barbara J. Little, pp. 167–175. University Press of Florida, Gainesville.

Mullins, Paul R.
2006   Racializing the Commonplace Landscape: An Archaeology of Urban Renewal Along the Color Line. *World Archaeology* 38(1): 60–71.

Nader, Laura
2001   Anthropology! Distinguished Lecture—2000. *American Anthropologist* 103(3): 609–620.

National Center for History in the Schools
1996   *National Standards for History*. Basic edition. University of California Press, Los Angeles.

Orser, Charles E., Jr.
2004   Archaeological Interpretation and the Irish Diasporic Community. In *Places in Mind: Public Archaeology as Applied Anthropology*, edited by P. A. Shackel and E. J. Chambers, pp. 171–191. Routledge, New York.

Pikirayi, Innocent
2006   Gold, Black Ivory, and Houses of Stone: Historical Archaeology in Africa. In *Historical Archaeology*, edited by Martin Hall and Stephen W. Silliman, pp. 230–250. Blackwell, Oxford.

Praetzellis, Mary, and Adrian Praetzellis (editors)
2004   Putting the "There" There: Historical Archaeologies of West Oakland. I-880 Cypress Freeway Replacement Project. Anthropological Studies Center, Sonoma State University. California Department of Transportation contract 04A0538, Task Order 15. Electronic document, http://www.sonoma.edu/asc/cypress/finalreport/index.htm, accessed June 15, 2006.

Preucel, Robert W.
2002   Writing the Pueblo Revolt. In *Archaeologies of the Pueblo Revolt: Identity, Meaning, and Renewal in the Pueblo World*, edited by Robert W. Preucel, pp. 3–29. University of New Mexico Press, Albuquerque.

Ramos, Maria, and David Duganne
2000   Exploring Public Perceptions and Attitudes about Archaeology. Prepared by

Harris Interactive for the Society for American Archaeology. Electronic document, http://www.cr.nps.gov/aad/pubs/Harris/index.htm, accessed July 25, 2005.

Rathje, William
2001   Integrated Archaeology: A Garbage Paradigm. In *Archaeologies of the Contemporary Past*, edited by Victor Buchli and Gavin Lucas, pp. 63–76. Routledge, New York.

Rosenzweig, Roy, and David Thelen
1998   *The Presence of the Past: Popular Uses of History in American Life*. Columbia University Press, New York.

Sahlins, Marshall
1999   What Is Anthropological Enlightenment? Some Lessons of the Twentieth Century. *Annual Review of Anthropology* 28:i–xxii.

Shackel, Paul A.
1993   *Personal Discipline and Material Culture: An Archaeology of Annapolis, Maryland, 1695–1870*. University of Tennessee Press, Knoxville.
1996   *Culture Change and the New Technology: An Archaeology of the Early American Industrial Era*. Plenum Press, New York.
2003   *Memory in Black and White: Race, Commemoration, and the Post-Bellum Landscape*. AltaMira Press, Walnut Creek, CA.

Shackel, Paul A., Paul R. Mullins, and Mark S. Warner (editors)
1998   *Annapolis Pasts: Historical Archaeology in Annapolis, Maryland*. University of Tennessee Press, Knoxville.

Singleton, Theresa A.
1999   An Introduction to African-American Archaeology. In *I, Too, Am America: Archaeological Studies of African-American Life*, edited by T. A. Singleton, pp. 1–17. University Press of Virginia, Charlottesville.

Sobel, Mechal
1987   *The World They Made Together, Black and White Values in Eighteenth-Century Virginia*. Princeton University Press, Princeton, NJ.

Timken, Barbara C.
1993   World Heritage Education: A Prototype for Teaching Young People. In *Archaeological Heritage Management*, pp. 92–99. ICOMOS International Scientific Symposium. 10th General Assembly, Sri Lanka. Colombo, Sri Lanka.

Trigger, Bruce
1989   *A History of Archaeological Thought*. Cambridge University Press, Cambridge.

Tutu, Desmond
2004   The Truth and Reconciliation Process—Restorative Justice. The Third Longford Lecture, organized by the Frank Longford Charitable Trust working in association with the Prison Reform Trust, at Church House Westminster, sponsored by the *Independent*. Electronic document, http://www.restorativejustice.org/articlesdb/articles/4253, accessed July 21, 2005.

Walker, Melanie
2001   Higher Education, Critical Professionalism and Educational Action Research. *Debates in Higher Education,* University College London. Electronic document, http://www.ucl.ac.uk/cishe/seminars/dhe_papers/MWpaper.doc, accessed July 25, 2005.

Weil, Stephen
1990   *Rethinking the Museum and Other Meditations.* Smithsonian Institution Press, Washington, DC.

Williamson, Tom
1998   Gentry Landscapes in a Much Older Land. *British Archaeology* 36.

Wylie, Alison
1994   Facts and Fictions: Writing Archaeology in a Different Voice. Reprinted in *Archaeological Theory: Progress or Posture?* edited by Iain M. Mackenzie, pp. 3–18. Avebury/Ashgate Publishing Company, Brookfield, VT.

Yamin, Rebecca (editor)
2001   Becoming New York: The Five Points Neighborhood. *Historical Archaeology* 35(3).

Zembylas, Michalinos, and Charalambos Vrasidas
2004   Emotion, Reason, and Information and Communication Technologies in Education: Some Issues in a Post-Emotional Society. *E-Learning* 1(1): 105–127.

Index

About the Author

Barbara J. Little is particularly interested in the ways in which archaeological places and collections are valued, recognized, and interpreted. She is the editor of *Public Benefits of Archaeology* (2002), a collection of viewpoints on the value of archaeology for the public. She coauthored, with Don Hardesty, *Assessing Site Significance: A Guide for Archaeologists and Historians* (2000), which explains the U. S. National Register process and use of the evaluation criteria and historic contexts. She is coeditor of *Heritage of Value, Archaeology of Renown: Reshaping Archaeological Assessment and Significance* (2005) along with Clay Mathers and Timothy Darvill. This collection is a call to the international archaeology profession to re-engage and reinvigorate discussions about site significance and public involvement. Barbara is also coeditor with Paul A. Shackel of the forthcoming *Archaeology as a Tool of Civic Engagement*. Barbara grew up in Pottstown, Pennsylvania, and got her B.A. in anthropology at Pennsylvania State University with a minor in science, technology, and society. Her M.A. and Ph.D. degrees in anthropology are from the State University of New York at Buffalo. She lives in Takoma Park, Maryland.